THE MODERN SCOTTISH THEATRE

by David Hutchison

with a Foreword by Christopher Small

Published by THE MOLENDINAR PRESS, Glasgow

The Molendinar Press
126 West Princes Street
Glasgow G4

This edition first published 1977

© David Hutchison
ISBN 0 904002 18 7 (UK edition)

**Made and printed in Great Britain by John G Eccles Ltd,
Inverness**

FOREWORD

A HISTORY OF THE MODERN SCOTTISH THEATRE— or one, indeed, of the Scottish theatre ancient and modern — would seem likely at first blush to be a short one; even, like the celebrated chapter on Snakes in the History of Iceland, to be encompassed in a single terse negative sentence. No one perhaps would in former times have gone quite so far as to say simply there is no such thing: but many even today might well wonder if there is enough of a Scottish theatre to make a study of.

David Hutchison's work, turning such dismissive thoughts upside down, is a substantial one, and not just in size but importance. It is one of those genuinely pioneering books which not only are the first to explore a subject but by exploring it define it, and even thereby help to bring it into being. A Scottish theatre is not the same thing as the mere occurrence of theatricals in Scotland, but exactly how it differs most of those interested in it — from many points of view — would find it hard to say. Even while talking about it they have been uncertain of the subject, and have indeed been anxious to know just what they were talking about. Mr Hutchison goes a long way to satisfying them: that is to say, he describes in a comprehensive and convincing way what the Scottish theatre is, in its various aspects, from its material arrangements to the more tricky matter of its individual spirit or national character; he tells how it has come into being; and he gives some idea at least of where it may be going. In the course of his narrative he shows us the matter in hand more clearly perhaps than anyone has done before, and why it is worth taking seriously. Argument about the Scottish theatre has been marked, often enough, by more enthusiasm than clarity; Mr Hutchison is an enthusiast of the more sober sort, who believes that if something is worth thinking about at all it is worth thinking about clearly.

Although this book deals with all aspects of the subject — the Scottish theatre as institution, as bricks and mortar, and as the history of different theatrical companies and enterprises in Scotland — the main emphasis is put on the development of writing for the theatre. There are perhaps three particular matters to comment upon here, each one having a historical connection with the others.

There is the point, well made by Mr Hutchison (and a reproach in the by-going to those directors of Scottish theatres who have too soon despaired of finding presentable new work in Scotland) that "good plays do not suddenly appear", but of course they grow out of a larger mass of the mediocre, the partially successful, even the downright bad. Looking towards the great and illustrious periods of the drama, we remember the masterpieces and forget the undergrowth of undistinguished stuff from which they sprung: only scholars wade through the lesser Elizabethans and Jacobeans above whom Marlowe, Shakespeare, Webster gloriously rose. Thus it may be said that the Scottish theatre, soberly assessed, is still at the early stage of providing the groundwork, the accumulation of experience, the chance of actual performance in many diverse forms, the comparisons and mutual stimulations of artistic association, and the encouragement of public interest, by which a real and powerful national drama may be nurtured. And it is certainly true that there is more of this ground-cultivation or foundation-laying going on in Scotland now than at any time in the past half-century or more.

A Scottish theatre may be about to burst into enlarged and heightened life; and the second point is that nearly all historical example indicates a connection between social and national stirabout in other fields and an active drama. It would not go too far to say that within limits the drama flourishes best in times of turbulence. It was — so at any rate many in the days of the Scottish National Players believed — Irish nationalism that gave birth to the Irish theatre; the corollary was that a similar theatrical life would arise in Scotland as part of the national renaissance. It did not really come about, at least when the word 'renaissance' was most in the air; but that very shortcoming can be taken as a reason for renewed expectation nowadays. For today national consciousness and national aspirations have spread abroad and taken hold with urgent political and economic consequences, in a way only the most starry-eyed or far-sighted (qualities more nearly akin than is usually admitted) could have dreamt possible in the twenties. In the midst of this renewed, widespread, indeed nation-wide upsurge, will not a national theatre have a field more fertile that it ever found before?

There are many signs already that it is so: enough, in fact, for a third consideration to become important. The kind of national drama which is chiefly a form of national self-congratulation is as sure a road as any to dullness, stagnation and the rest of the seven deadly institutional virtues (the others are safeness, regularity, respectability, orthodoxy, and, finally, censorship). The example of National Socialist theatre is too odious to be mentioned; but what has happened in Ireland ought to be as much warning as inspiration — and it mustn't ever be forgotten that Synge and O'Casey themselves, the chief heroes of the Irish National drama, were anathema accursed to all good right-thinking little nationalists in their day. An even greater hero (also frequently invoked as a towering exemplar) is Ibsen, who, like many another man of genius subsequently enshrined in a national pantheon, had to shake the dust of Norway off his feet before turning and telling his countrymen, the national-patriots being first on the list, just what he thought of them.

All kinds of emotion, every imaginable exercise of the intellect can contribute to the life of the drama, but one in particular gives it energy and stimulus to development: criticism, the peculiar way in which the art of the theatre performs the function described by Hamlet, of holding up the mirror to nature. This is not the place to inquire into that subtle and even mysterious operation, except to observe that it is something Scots ought especially to understand and relish. They *ought* to, for reasons clear enough in the cultural history of the past four hundred years; though for the very same reasons they have until lately found it difficult or unnecessary.

Mr Hutchison, like many others looking backward over Scotland's barren theatrical landscape, has laid some of the blame for its infertility upon the Kirk, and obviously it is true. When any institution has had the influence on a nation's culture that the Reformed Church has had in Scotland, it must take some blame — or credit — for everything in that culture or excluded from it; and the theatre, condemned as the home of Belial, has every reason to count itself among the chief casualties of Presbyterianism. But simply to condemn a popular activity like play-going and play-acting is not as a rule to destroy it; even when condemnation is followed (as it was in the England of the Commonwealth) by active suppression, the accursed thing is all too apt to spring up again later, more unregenerate than ever. The more effective method of turning a people from what are thought to be evil ways is to offer them another not too different path, an acceptable substitute: and that is precisely what the Kirk did.

When we take a retrospect of Scotland's ecclesiastical and theological history of four centuries and see the furious contentions and schisms, the confrontations and departures, the overflowing polemics with which they have been marked; when we consider the great mass of learning and talent, the personal energies, the scale of emotions from extremes of hatred to extremes of love, concentrated and poured out in unceasing commentary on everything on earth and beyond it from the pulpits of Scotland during most of this time, we need not wonder that the nation took the disappearance of mere secular drama without protest or regret. Who, when the churches were packed and ten thousand preachers were debating the issues of Heaven and Hell each Sabbath day, would bother with a paltry playhouse?

But the churches are packed no longer, even if they can still muster a slightly better weekly total than the theatres. Let neither side be offended by the comparison; for if things have changed nowadays, so that church-going as well as theatre-going is a minority activity, it may also be easier to see that what is to be gained by both is not in truth in competition at all, and may in part be mutually encouraging. The expectation that the Church in one of its functions is the critic of society as well as of individuals is one deeply rooted in Scottish religious tradition; it brings the ideal of preaching (Lord knows, it is not often more than an ideal) very close in object and even in mode of operation to the poetry which is the unacknowledged legislation of the world. We certainly don't want a theatre that preaches — in the depressing sense of unprofitable exhortation which has come to be associated with the word — and we no longer want preachers who preach. But a theatre which treats of all the affairs of men that are reckoned the legitimate province of preaching — national, social, and individual — and which does it by its own means, including spectacle and movement and music and song, and all the infinite possibilities encompassed by the formula of 'imitation of an action'; which uses laughter and mere playfulness and appeals to the senses as well as to the intellect; but which also has some of the bite, the attack, the zeal for truth and the want of respect for persons of Scottish homiletics at their most combative: that, I think, is the kind of theatre that will appeal best to us, and especially perhaps in our present excited, confused, but by no means unhopeful national situation.

Mr Hutchison reminds us, very sensibly, that a National Theatre does not necessarily mean a single institution or building; perhaps, looking over our shoulders at the imperial ambitions and sway of the foundation south of the border, we may well feel that as something to be avoided. A National Theatre which is rather an assembly of companies, of diverse composition and methods and presenting a very varied repertoire, may be more practicable and desirable; it is one which we almost have the makings of already. The chief ingredient missing is of course the one this book is largely concerned with, the Scottish drama which would form a common possession of all. Whether the early shoots and flowers described here will go on growing, and even in due course produce something truly great and astonishing, it is impossible to say. Some of the conditions are right, and the appearance of this book is in itself evidence of them. It tells us where we are and so helps to make us think where we just might be going.

Christopher Small
Glasgow, April 1977

ACKNOWLEDGEMENTS

THE AUTHOR WOULD LIKE TO EXPRESS HIS THANKS to the following for their assistance: Mrs W. Bannister, the late James Gibson, John Hill, W. H. D. Joss, Moultrie Kelsall, Donald McBean, Mrs Grace McChlery, Robert McLellan, Mrs G. Malloch, Mrs H. Russell, Miss Jean Taylor Smith, Andrew Stewart, and Mrs W. Webster.

The following have also been very helpful: the artistic directors of the Scottish repertory theatres, town clerks, burgh librarians, archivists and police departments in various parts of Scotland, also S.C.O.T.T.S., the St. Giles Press, Derek Glynne Ltd., and Baillie's Library, the Mitchell Library and the University Library in Glasgow, as well as Ayr County Council library service.

This book is based on work done for an M.Litt. thesis at the University of Glasgow, and no such work could be completed without the help of a large number of people too numerous to mention here individually. However, a particular debt must be acknowledged to Professor James Arnott whose own knowledge and constant advice have been invaluable.

I must also express my thanks to Simon Berry of The Molendinar Press, whose constant championing of the general reader has exerted a powerful and salutary discipline throughout the writing of this book, and to Mrs Cathy Brown and Mrs Margaret Gray, who have coped with innumerable drafts and revisions in handwriting that often leaves much to be desired.

The publisher would like to thank the Duncan Macrae Memorial Trust Fund for their assistance in the publication of this book, and also to all those who gave their time freely to read and comment upon the manuscript.

CONTENTS

A NOTE ON THE TEXT

The date and place of first production is given in brackets after the title of each play discussed. The source of quotations is generally acknowledged within the text or in brackets at the end of quotations. Many of the theatres mentioned and the magazines cited are no longer in existence; indeed, many of the plays discussed exist only in typescript. For further information the reader is directed to the Appendices.

CHAPTER ONE
Introduction

THEATRE-GOING IS A MINORITY PURSUIT and only a very small proportion of people ever show an active interest in it. Nonetheless, many countries seem to want national theatres and appear through the agency of Governments to be prepared to pay for them. The most obvious recent example of this principle at work is the National Theatre in London which opened its partially completed building in the spring of 1976. During the twentieth century in Britain we have witnessed not only a long and arduous campaign to establish the National Theatre, but also the establishment in Ireland of an Irish National Theatre, the Abbey, in Dublin, which in 1924 became the first state-subsidised theatre in the English-speaking world.

We have also seen, and this is what we shall be concerned with here, a succession of attempts to establish a national theatre in Scotland. Admittedly we have not witnessed such intense devotion to the erection of a national theatre building, although such a building has been suggested from time to time. What we have had since the beginning of the century is a growth in the amount of serious theatrical activity in Scotland and the emergence of a group of writers who see themselves as writing for the Scottish, as opposed to or as well as the English theatre and expressing in their work things they believe are essentially though not exclusively Scottish. This book is an attempt to give an account of the achievement to date, in the hope that by perceiving clearly where we have now arrived we can perhaps speculate intelligently on where we shall be going.

There are three distinct phases in the life of Scottish theatre this century. First of all there is the period at the turn of the nineteenth into the twentieth century, when the distinction between theatre as a pleasant way of passing an evening and theatre as an art form able to make some serious comment on life was emerging throughout Europe. These two different kinds of theatre we have today reflect in the distinction — not entirely watertight — between commercial and non-commercial. We shall be looking in detail at one of the first theatres in the United Kingdom which sought to promote theatre as art, the

1

Glasgow Repertory. It ought to be much better known, for it was one of the great pioneers of the repertory theatre movement.

Secondly there is the period following on the First World War, a conflagration that brought the Glasgow Repertory Theatre to an abrupt end just as it was beginning to establish itself. The inter-war period is essentially that of the amateur theatre in Scotland. The commercial theatre was still there, of course, though reduced in circumstances by the ravages of the cinema, but the burden of developing a Scottish theatre passed from the Glasgow Repertory to the amateur movement, and we shall be considering how that movement — and in particular the Scottish National Players — faced up to the rather daunting responsibility.

The Second World War did not prove as calamitous for the Scottish theatre and the pattern of repertory theatres we now have in Scotland, the first traces of which were obvious before 1939 in Perth and during that year in Dundee, took recognisable shape with the establishment of the Glasgow Citizens' Theatre in 1943 and the Gateway in Edinburgh in 1946. The growth of repertory theatre — which forms our third phase — has continued since then and still continues. At the same time the commercial theatre has entered a period of rapid decline and we have seen the municipalisation of most of the commercial theatre buildings that have kept their doors open. This is a complete reversal of the position at the beginning of the century when the commercial theatre was flourishing and the repertory theatre was struggling for existence. As we shall see, there are a large number of factors involved in such a turn of events, not least the development of cinema and television and the acceptance of the idea that theatre is something to be subsidized from public funds.

As we shall be looking at the changing pattern of theatrical facilities, so too we shall be considering the changing pattern of Scottish writing, from its faltering steps on the stage of the old Royalty Theatre, where the Glasgow Repertory performed, to the much more confident measures of the outstanding Scottish playwright, James Bridie, and the extremely varied paces of our recent Scottish dramatists. Throughout, the aim will be to evaluate their work in theatrical terms and to ascertain how far it approaches the oft-declared objective of rendering Scottish life in all its variety on the stage.

Scottish dramatists have had to cope with the great problem of the absence of a significant dramatic tradition within which to work. As we examine how they have dealt with this situation, the emphasis will be on those writers who operated in the Scottish theatre, or at least had it as a base. This means that the plays of James Barrie will not be dealt with: Barrie worked for the English theatre within its traditions, making — it should be stressed — a distinguished contribution to it. Scotland does not figure largely in his writing for the stage (although one can argue that Barrie's sentimentality is essentially Scottish, for it is at the heart of the 'kailyard school' of prose writers which continues to this day in publications like *The People's Friend*), and when it does feature it is a rural Scotland, a quaint Scotland, a Scotland where strange and mysterious things can happen. It has to be added immediately, however, that although Barrie worked within the English theatre and had his major successes there, he remains extremely popular with Scottish audiences. Both the Gateway and the Citizens' companies performed his work regularly in the forties and fifties, while Pitlochry Festival Theatre has always had a particular affection for him. For all Barrie's success stemmed from his being an expatriate, audiences north of the border still respond to his plays as much as do metropolitan audiences.

Barrie's success stemmed from the fact that he forsook his Scottish background and consequently embarked on a career in London which was extremely rewarding financially. The irony of his success is perhaps a little depressing, for while it is probably true that he made the right choice in terms of acclaim and money, it is also true that his career illustrates something of the difficulties in the way of the Scottish dramatist who chooses to write mainly about his own country. That so many writers have chosen to work in the Scottish theatre is however an indication of the strength of belief that there is something important to be done in Scotland which could not be done elsewhere.

CHAPTER TWO
Setting the Scene

AT THE END OF THE NINETEENTH CENTURY Scotland had more theatres than at any previous time in her history. There were some twenty-five theatre buildings, most of them in the cities but also to be found in such centres as Coatbridge, Greenock, Inverness, Paisley and Leith. In addition, there was a large number of music halls — Glasgow, for example, had about half a dozen.

Despite their strength in numbers, the Scottish theatres of this period were almost entirely dependent for their presentations on touring companies based in London, which brought the latest metropolitan successes to the rest of the country. The *Glasgow Herald* (whose leader writers took a considerable interest in matters theatrical) commented frequently in the 1890s about the way in which London "gives the law to the provinces" and the highly centralized organisation of the theatre. If we examine the records of performances during the period in question we can see clearly what the *Herald* was concerned about. In Glasgow and in Edinburgh innumerable London-based companies, famous and obscure, occupied the theatres — Henry Irving's Lyceum Company, Beerbohm Tree's Company, Charles H. Hawtrey's Company, Hubert O'Grady's Irish Company, John Hare and Company, F. W. Benson and his Shakespeare Company, Mr D'Oyly Carte's Opera Company and the Carl Rosa Opera Company, to name a few. In accordance with the practice which began in the nineteenth century, and continues to this day, companies were specially formed for the presentation of particular plays. In October 1893, for example, the Theatre Royal, Glasgow, was occupied by the Morocco Bound Burlesque Company, giving performances of Arthur Brunscombe's *Morocco Bound*, following its premiere at the Shaftesbury Theatre, London, in April of the same year (a good example of the way in which a London success was thereafter trundled round the provinces). While in April 1882 the Royalty in Glasgow had a performance of *H.M.S. Pinafore* by the Children's Pinafore Company.

Scotland has its share of performances of the current

4

successes by writers such as H. J. Byron, T. W. Robertson, Tom Taylor and Dion Boucicault. Comedies abounded, usually publicised in the kind of terms reserved for the world of show business — *Betsy* was advertised as "the enormously successful farcical comedy" for Edinburgh's Theatre Royal in 1891, and *Love in all Corners* "the screaming farce" according to a programme at Glasgow's Gaiety in 1880. Full-length plays were usually prefaced by one-act comediettas, and sometimes performances concluded with similar short pieces, even although the effect might on occasion be incongruous — a performance of *Othello* in the Glasgow Gaiety in 1881 was advertised as "concluding each evening with a favourite farce", and in 1887 at the Grand in Glasgow the Reverend E. Moore's "great tragedy" *The Gamester* was accompanied by "the laughable farce" *A Fish Out of Water*. The Victorians liked plenty of variety during their evening at the theatre — the programme for a performance of *As You Like It* at the Royalty, Glasgow, in 1882 tells us: "On this occasion Mr W. H. Pennington will recite *The Charge of the Light Brigade*"!

Glasgow and Edinburgh had their fair share of Shakespearean performances. Irving visited both cities with his company on a large number of occasions, and his was only one of several troupes on the road. Also during this period there were innumerable performances of stage adaptations from the novels of Scott, and Scottish theatres not surprisingly saw a large number of performances of *Rob Roy*, *The Lady of the Lake* and *Marmion*. These performances, which continued into the early twentieth century and appear to have persisted longer north of the border than south of it, were sometimes given by travelling companies from England and sometimes by companies which were organised in Scotland by a theatrical management such as Howard and Wyndham.

Some theatregoers of the time were under no illusion as to the worth of such 'Scottish' plays. As the *Glasgow Herald* commented:

> *Apart, however, from the Bailie, the* 'Rob Roy' *not of Scott but of the present day, is simply a Scotch Showpiece for the delectation of England and American tourists — the same tourists who find the Dungeon of Buchan "so picturesque" and, sustained by aereated beverages and faith in dear delightful Mr Barrie, try through the Window in Thrums to witness the tragedy of humble Scots life.*

*Major Galbraith and Andrew Fairservice have been
converted into sheer "flagrant examples" of the mischief
done by Scotch drink, while Diana Vernon and Francis
Osbaldistone, with their weakness for bursting into song at
the most critical moments, are simply walking illustrations
of the beauty of Scotch melody.* (18 May 1895)

But there were more hopeful signs towards the end of the
century. A series of performances of classical English drama in
Glasgow in 1899 under the auspices of the General Committee of
The Classical English Drama, was very successful, thus indicating
the growth in public appreciation of drama. The Puritan dislike
of the theatre, however, was still very much alive. The columns
of the *Glasgow Herald* were taken up in 1899 with a protracted
correspondence entitled "The Church and the Theatre", in
which various individuals argued for and against the proposition
that the theatre is an abomination of the devil. It is interesting
to note that nine years previously the same paper had argued
that such prejudice no longer existed in Scotland.

We do find some traces of a Scottish drama during the
period — at least of plays written by Scotsmen being performed.
In 1894, for example, A. W. Yuill's farce *Married by Proxy* was
given its first performance in Greenock, followed by a London
production a year later. In October 1895 the lessee and
manager of the Grand Theatre, Glasgow, Ernest Stevens, had
his play *Scots Wha Hae wi' Wallace Bled* premiered. Stevens
followed this with two other plays, *Ivanhoe* and *For Bonnie
Scotland*. These plays were praised at the time, but in terms
which place them in the company of the hundreds of other
forgettable dramas and melodramas of the period. In June 1896
a play called *Robert Burns* was presented at the Royal in
Glasgow. According to a report in the *Glasgow Theatrical
Annual* the play had been "produced for the first time a week
before in Edinburgh. It was a failure. Fortunately for the author
his name was not revealed". It has to be admitted that it is
difficult to find much in the way of Scottish drama in the
professional theatre at this time. Scots were writing plays, but
the evidence suggests that for the most part they were merely
imitating the plays which were being presented in London and,
as most of these plays had little merit, so the Scottish ones do
not seem to have had much either.

The amateur drama movement had not reached the peak it was to attain in the second quarter of the twentieth century in Scotland, but it still seems to have been reasonably active. If we turn to it in the hope of finding hints of an emerging national drama, however, we are going to be disappointed. The amateur theatre appears to have followed in the footsteps of the professional one, with only the occasional Scottish play. It is perhaps worth mentioning that in 1893 the Glasgow Junior Club put on a play by their stage manager, W. Graham Moffat, entitled *The Fifth Act or A Drama Rehearsed*, which appears to have been an apprentice piece by the author of *Bunty Pulls the Strings*. That play, in some ways an early blow in the equality for women campaign, was premiered in London in 1911 and ran for over six hundred performances. It was something of a family affair, for the company with which Moffat toured for years thereafter included the author, his wife, his daughter, two of his brothers and his sister. Moffat wrote several other successful if equally lightweight plays and then retired to pursue his interest in psychic research. *The Prompter*, a short-lived magazine devoted — initially at any rate — to the amateur theatre in Scotland, described *The Fifth Act* as a "very clever little piece".

It is arguable that the pantomime in Scotland at this time was much more Scottish than anything else in the theatre and, for all that pantomime as such is outside the scope of this study, we ought to give some attention to it in passing. Although Glasgow did often copy London successes, there seem to have been deliberate efforts to produce scripts with a local flavour. This applies in particular to the pantomimes Fred Locke wrote for the Royal Princess's, now the Glasgow Citizens' Theatre: Robinson Crusoe, for example, departs from the Broomielaw, and Dick Whittington finds his fortune in Glasghu; in *Mother Hubbard*, performed in the 1888-9 season, we find that the localization of the story extends to the introduction of characters such as Sir Kelvin Grove, references to the local Gas Company and the use of Scots vernacular for characters on the lower rungs of the social scale. In Edinburgh Howard and Wyndham presented a regular series of pantomimes at the Royal and here too local references were common. In *Sinbad the Sailor*, performed in the 1890-91 season, fun is derived from various local railway schemes and derogatory comments are made about the quality of the Corporation gas.

According to the *Glasgow Harlequin* — a periodical which flourished briefly in the city during the 1895-96 season — pantomime had a regular clientele of sixty thousand people weekly. The *Harlequin* itself ran a competition in which readers were asked to nominate their choice of best performer of the season. The prize, a large cake, went to Percy Milton for his performance in *Robinson Crusoe* at the Grand. Some nine thousand votes were cast, which — even allowing for double voting — demonstrates the immense popularity of pantomime. In the production of pantomimes no expense seems to have been spared. F. W. Wyndham, in an interview with the *Harlequin*, is reported as saying that a production of his cost between three and four thousand pounds, independent of salaries for the two hundred and fifty people employed.

Another form of theatre very popular at this time was the music hall, where a native tradition of Scotch comics, many of whom drew their material from urban working-class life, was being built up. This tradition, which was very much linked with the pantomime, is also outside the scope of this book, but it does appear that the only substantial Scottish contribution to the theatre during the period was made on the pantomime stage and in the music halls. It would be wrong then to pass on without stressing the importance of this contribution. It is one from which many Scottish actors have drawn sustenance, and indeed there has been and remains a two-way traffic between the theatre and pantomime and what is left of the music hall tradition in the variety theatre. In our own time Stanley Baxter began in the theatre and then moved into pantomime and variety, where his undoubted comic talent has blossomed. Rikki Fulton has made the journey the other way round. The actor who best exploited both traditions, and was equally at home in both, was of course Duncan Macrae. He began as an actor, discovered his comic genius, and brought it to fruition in both pantomime and straight theatre.

There does not, however, seem to have been much evidence of Scottish dramatic art at the end of the nineteenth century. Several reasons can be suggested. The first and most obvious is that Scotland had no dramatic or theatrical traditions worth talking of. Whereas the English theatre stretched back from the present day through the Elizabethan and Jacobean playwrights to the medieval drama, the Scottish dramatic inheritance is a much less substantial one. There are ample records of medieval plays being produced in Scotland, and then there is Sir David Lindsay's marvellously accomplished *Satire of the Three Estates*, presented at Cupar in 1552, but the departure of the Court for London in 1603 and the attitude of the Presbyterian Church prevented further possible developments. The Church did not, to be fair, attack the theatre immediately after the Reformation. Indeed, for a time it sponsored plays which were vehicles for anti-Catholic propaganda, John Knox himself attending several performances of such works. Plays on biblical subjects were also performed. However, the Kirk soon banned Robin Hood plays, and in 1575 the General Assembly went further, and banned "clerk-plays or comedies based upon the canonical scriptures". While the Court remained in Edinburgh it supported the theatre (which probably incensed the theatre's enemies even more), but on the death of Elizabeth I and the consequent Union of the Crowns this support disappeared. For the next hundred years or so theatrical activity was sparse, although performances by visiting English companies did take place. When the Duke of York came to reside in Scotland in 1679 he brought a company drawn from the London playhouses to Edinburgh, and they appear to have remained for several years.

During the eighteenth century efforts were made to start theatres in the face of religious opposition, particularly in Edinburgh, and in 1736 Allan Ramsay, the author of the pastoral *The Gentle Shepherd* (first performed in 1729), managed to open Edinburgh's — and Scotland's — first regular theatre in Carrubber's Close. But it was forced to close the following year as a consequence of the Government's licensing act, a measure which was designed to deal with with political satire in the London theatre and had no relevance to the Scottish situation.

In Glasgow similar attempts to initiate theatrical activity often met with mixed reactions and on occasions a violent end. George Ann Bellamy in her *Apology* gives an account of the destruction of a theatre in Glasgow in 1764 by a mob influenced by a Methodist preacher. The theatre had been constructed, according to her account of the matter, on the specific under-standing that she and her company would act in it; but before they could set foot on the boards the mob had set fire to it.

It is obvious that an atmosphere where such things could happen was, to say the least, a discouragement. Theatrical activity did continue, however, in both the major cities and theatres began to be established on a permanent basis towards the end of the eighteenth century. Edinburgh's first Theatre Royal received its royal patent in 1767 and Glasgow's Dunlop Street theatre, latterly known as the Royal, opened in 1782. But it will be clear that during most of that century theatre had a very precarious hold on Scottish life.

It was extremely improbable that authors would continue to write for a scarcely existent theatre; consequently few plays appeared, even fewer of merit. It is easy to abuse such plays as were written in eighteenth-century Scotland, but what must be borne in mind is that their authors had no theatrical or dramatic tradition within which they could work.

Such writers as did appear soon realized that if they were to succeed they would have to aim at the London market. Indeed this had been realized in the seventeenth century by Thomas St. Serfe (or Sydserf) whose play *Tarugo's Wiles* was premiered in London in 1667, and was the first Scottish play to be premiered in the capital. The moral has been taken by Scottish dramatists since, most conspicuously by James Barrie. In the eighteenth century a writer as moderately successful in Scotland as John Home sought London premieres. The financial inducement was obvious: *Douglas*, Home's most famous play — which is extremely difficult even to read nowadays, despite the fact that it is supposed to have roused a member of the first night audience to shout "whaur's yer Wully Shakespeare noo?" — was extremely successful in Edinburgh where it was premiered in 1756. But that success meant only a six-night run initially. There was another inducement to look south: as a consequence of the play being performed Home found himself summoned before the Presbytery of Haddington and six months after *Douglas* had its premiere he resigned his post as minister at Athelstaneford.

It might be thought that when, in the early nineteenth century, some Scottish stock companies were formed and theatre in Scotland began to expand, the opportunity would thus have been provided for new writers to develop. But at that time the pitiable economic position of the dramatist would have been a major disincentive. By later in the century, when the earning power of the playwright had increased, Scotland like the rest of the provinces had become so dependent on London for theatrical fare that a Scottish dramatic tradition was unlikely to emerge.

The almost complete absence of Scots plays from the nineteenth-century Scottish stage, and the complete absence of any play of merit, can be attributed to economic factors, the dominance of London and the lack of a theatrical tradition. There was the consequent lack of a dramatic tradition within which playwrights could work, and against the achievements of which they could measure their own efforts. Good writers, almost without exception, spring from a tradition of writing, which need not be a very long one but which must have both identity and vitality. Such a tradition has only just begun to exist in Scotland this century.

If we look at contemporary opinions of the Scottish theatrical situation at the end of the nineteenth century, we discover unsurprisingly that some observers were convinced that a dramatic tradition could not be fostered in Scotland. In 1890 the *Glasgow Herald* printed a review of the published text of Charles Waddie's play, *Wallace or the Battle of Stirling Bridge*, which was not to be performed until it was given a presentation in Stirling in 1898. The reviewer poses the question "Why is the dramatic muse silent in Scotland?" and quotes Waddie as suggesting this is because there is no resident dramatic company in Scotland. The reviewer says there is no silence in Scotland, for there is no muse to be silent, rather "The poetic genius of Scotland is entirely and intensely lyrical". This statement is obviously question-begging, but it does illustrate the pessimism that some Scots felt at that time when contemplating their nation's dramatic literature. The commentator eighty years on can fortunately take a much more sanguine view of the Scottish dramatic and theatrical achievement. To the foundations of this achievement we now must turn.

CHAPTER THREE
The Glasgow Repertory Company

THEATRE WAS A GROWTH INDUSTRY IN SCOTLAND at the beginning of this century, as the figures below demonstrate.

NUMBER OF THEATRES IN SCOTLAND

	Total	Aberdeen	Dundee	Edinburgh	Glasgow
1900	32	2	3	5	10
1910	53	3	6	7	15

The first decade of the century was marked by an upsurge in theatre building, particularly in Glasgow: the King's opened in 1904, the Pavilion the same year, the Alhambra in 1910, the Lyceum in 1900, the Palace in 1904, the Coliseum in 1905 and Hengler's in 1905. It is interesting to note that the King's, Pavilion and Alhambra were large theatres in the centre of the city while most of the others were music halls serving their immediate locality. In the event it was the music halls that suffered most as a consequence of the advances of the cinema: from being neighbourhood music halls they became neighbourhood cinemas, a transition that was not so readily open to the city centre theatres. But that transition was yet to come, and in 1906 the Glasgow *Evening Citizen* could inform a curious reader that the total seating capacity of the city's theatres was 29,000.

Elsewhere in Scotland theatres were also being opened: the Gaiety in Ayr (1902), the Grand (1903) and the Electric (1910) in Falkirk, the Empire (1903) and King's (1909) in Dundee, the King's (1906) in Edinburgh, the Empire (1903) in Greenock, the Hippodrome (1907) in Hamilton and the King's (1904) in Kirkcaldy. The confidence of the managements of the time can be seen in the architecture of the buildings they erected. Those that are still with us, for example the King's in Glasgow and the King's in Edinburgh, are substantial and attractive edifices. When they opened, press comment emphasised their sumptuousness, comfort and pleasing decor.

Against this background there was established in Glasgow a repertory company whose work, although it was short-lived, is of great importance in the history of Scottish theatre. This was the Glasgow Repertory Company. But before examining its development in detail it would perhaps be helpful to say something about the early years of the repertory theatre movement.

Theatrical taste in Britain had, during the second half of the nineteenth century, undergone some changes. In the middle of the century despite the presence of some actors of considerable talent the stage was largely given over to work of little substance which depended for an impact on empty rhetoric and vulgar spectacle. The audience was a rowdy and ill-mannered one which did not hesitate to show its feelings. The upper classes and the by now more important business classes preferred either to stay at home or to patronize the opera.

Slowly taste began to improve: T. W. Robertson's plays, which were realistic and contemporary and avoided the wilder flights of melodrama, re-established the theatre as a vehicle worthy of a serious writer's attentions; the audience began to draw from the ranks of commerce and even the upper classes felt that they could once again be seen in a theatre; theatre buildings became more comfortable and the rowdier element which had predominated in the middle of the century found itself being squeezed out by economic and social pressures.

It would be inaccurate to claim that by the end of the nineteenth century there was a large audience intent on serious theatre. This was not the case, as the previous chapter makes clear. But there was a largely middle-class audience which considered theatre-going respectable, although its taste did not extend very far beyond rather light fare and it had a fatal inclination towards the sentimental. It might accept plays that dealt with contemporary life provided they did not bite too deeply. Where a writer like Ibsen was concerned, however, it was quite clear that most members of the audience wanted nothing to do with him.

The first Ibsen performance in London was in 1880 when a version of *Pillars of Society* was given (under the title of *Quicksands*). Performances of other Ibsen plays followed (including a version of *A Doll's House* by Henry Arthur Jones entitled *Breaking a Butterfly* which had a happy ending). Inevitably the presentation of work so different from what was normally being seen on the English stage led to a hotly contested debate, with William Archer, the Scottish journalist who left the *Edinburgh Evening News* for London in 1878, acting as the champion of the New Drama and Clement Scott of the *Daily Telegraph* fighting for a drama that did not explore the darker sides of life but concentrated on telling the audience pleasing stories. In this conflict can be seen the beginnings of the split between a theatre offering harmless and pleasing entertainment and one seeking to explore life in all its complexity. The split is mirrored, if rather crudely, in the distinction between commercial and non-commercial theatre.

In 1891 J. T. Grein founded the Independent Theatre of London "to give special performances of plays which have a literary and artistic rather than a commercial value". The Independent Theatre's first production was a private one of Ibsen's *Ghosts* which aroused tremendous fury among the critics. Grein was also to be responsible for the first London production of a play by Shaw, *Widowers' Houses* in 1892. In 1899 the Stage Society, London, was founded with similar aims to those of the Independent Theatre. It was responsible for Sunday evening performances in West End theatres of plays that lacked commercial appeal. Shaw benefited from its work, as did numerous foreign dramatists, including Hauptmann and Pirandello.

The principle of West End performances for non-commercial plays was taken up in the seasons at the Court Theatre from 1904 to 1907 organised by John Vedrenne, the theatre manager, and Harley Granville Barker, the producer. In this case plays were given a run of three matinees a week for a fortnight. Matinees were a matter of necessity, for only thus was it possible to secure West End actors who were playing elsewhere in the evenings. The Vedrenne-Barker seasons included work by Shaw, Galsworthy, Hauptmann, Maeterlinck and Euripides, and could be regarded as the first repertory seasons in Britain.

True repertory is a system in which several plays are performed in any one week and others are being rehearsed in preparation for insertion into the programme, so that ultimately the company might have a number of plays available for performance in various permutations. It is not a system that has been much employed in this country, although the National Theatre and the Royal Shakespeare Company attempt it on a limited scale. Rather our repertory theatres tend to present each play for a fortnight or three weeks. After that period the production is not usually retained. The distinction between this system and the one employed in the commercial theatre is that in repertory the long run is being avoided as a matter of deliberate policy, whereas in the commercial it is sought as the way to financial success.

After the Court seasons there were other short-lived ventures of a similar kind in London, but it was from elsewhere in Britain that the impetus now came. Miss A. E. Horniman, who had been responsible for the building and equipping of the Abbey Theatre in Dublin, which after its opening in 1904 was the focal point of the revival in the Irish drama, acquired the Gaiety Theatre in Manchester and in 1908 opened it as a repertory theatre. The venture continued until 1917 and over two hundred plays were performed, half of them for the first time. The repertoire included work by the so-called Manchester school — Harold Brighouse, Stanley Houghton and Allen Monkhouse — as well as work by other British and foreign contemporary playwrights. Among the producers was Lewis Casson, who in fact joined the Glasgow Repertory Theatre after a spell in Manchester, and among Miss Horniman's associates at the time she was contemplating purchasing the Gaiety was Alfred Wareing.

Wareing was born at Greenwich in 1876. He gave up a career in the book trade for the theatre, beginning as an advance agent for F. R. Benson's company. From there he moved on to work for several other eminent actor managers and, while Company Manager for Beerbohm Tree on a visit to Dublin in 1906, he became interested in the work of the Abbey Theatre. Wareing was so impressed by the performances he saw that he arranged a tour for the Irish Players in Britain — which took in Aberdeen, Edinburgh and Glasgow as well as several other venues south of the border.

Wareing's involvement with the Irish Players and with Miss Horniman led directly to his developing the scheme for the establishment of a Repertory Theatre in Glasgow, of which venture he was to be managing director for most of its existence. When war brought the Rep. to a finish Wareing sought to enlist, but his deafness prevented him from doing so and he passed the next four years in various rather bedraggled theatrical enterprises. In 1918 he initiated a scheme for a theatre company, similar to the Glasgow Repertory, at the Theatre Royal, Huddersfield. For thirteen years he sought to alternate popular successes and more demanding fare, to some effect, but ultimately this venture also came to an end. The rest of Wareing's life until his death in 1942 was spent as a librarian in Stratford, first for the Memorial Theatre, then for the Borough, and in drawing up and promoting the scheme for the League of Audiences, the aim of which was to secure public subsidy for the performing arts. The scheme was an important factor in the formation of the Council for the Encouragement of Music and the Arts in 1940 and ultimately in the establishment of the Arts Council in 1946.

The Glasgow Repertory Company was established in 1909, but before that time there were signs of an increased interest in serious theatre in Scotland. Amateur dramatic clubs were being formed — the Glasgow Amateur Dramatic Company, for example, was formed in 1907. In 1908 the Glasgow Stage Society, formed for the purpose of fostering interest in literary drama in Glasgow and district, held its first meeting at which a lecture was delivered by Mr Frederick Whelan of the Stage Society, London, on the New Drama in the course of which he argued for "plays about English and Scottish life written by men who knew the life of the English and Scottish people".

In 1909, as a result of the efforts of Wareing and several prominent Glasgow citizens, a company was established. A meeting was held on 19 February at which Wareing explained his proposal to start a citizens' theatre in Glasgow and thus make the city theatrically independent of London. The enterprise was to be started with a capital of £2,000, one thousand of which would be called up. It was estimated by Wareing that it would cost £240 per week to run the theatre.

By the middle of March plans had been announced for a first season which was to commence at the beginning of April and the prospectus of Scottish Playgoers Ltd. issued:

> *The objects of the company include the establishment in Glasgow of a Repertory Theatre . . . the organisation of a stock company . . . and the encouragement of the initiation and development of purely Scottish drama by providing a stage and acting company which will be peculiarly adapted for the production of plays national in character, written by Scottish men and women of letters.* (Glasgow Herald, 19 March 1909)

The directors of the company were Professor W. MacNeile Dixon, the distinguished Professor of English at Glasgow University, Deacon Convenor Andrew Macdonald a leading businessman who acted as chairman, Neil Munro the journalist and writer, Professor J. S. Phillimore who held the chair of Humanity at Glasgow, J. W. Robb an accountant, and Alfred Wareing. They decided, in fact, to start the company with a capital of £3,000 in £1 shares, one thousand pounds more than had originally been announced, of which two thousand were offered for subscription. In point of fact only one thousand of these had been taken up when the company began operations in the Royalty Theatre in Sauchiehall Street, on the site of which the South of Scotland Electricity Board showroom now stands. The theatre had been leased for eighty pounds per week from Howard and Wyndham with all the profits from bars, cloakrooms and programme sales remaining with the proprietors.

It is important to realise that those who worked for the establishment of a peculiarly Scottish theatre had constantly before them the example of the Abbey Theatre in Dublin, where a distinctive Irish drama was in the process of being created. The achievements of the Irish drama were constantly invoked in all that was written about the Glasgow Rep., and on the death of J. M. Synge in 1909 the *Glasgow Herald* commented that the country was moving towards "the establishment of a Scottish theatre equal to the Irish one in national spirit and possibly superior to it in breadth of artistic horizon". Later on, when things were not going very well for the Rep., the writer of a letter to the same paper also invoked the Irish example and criticised the company for not emulating the Abbey.

In the souvenir programme for the opening season in 1909 a great deal of emphasis was put on the ensemble method the company was to adopt:

Playwrights have ceased to turn out work of the joiner's shop order — no longer do they remember they must fit 'the leads', 'the juveniles', 'the old men', 'the comedians', 'the responsibles', 'the first and second walking gentleman', 'the utility' and 'the chambermaids'. The most modern dramatic authors write for no particular actor or actress and when the play comes to be produced London is searched for a cast that shall realise all the author hopes to get out of his work . . . In the programme presented by the Scottish Playgoers Company the names of ultra-modern dramatists will be found: Bernard Shaw, John Galsworthy, and Arnold Bennett have thrown off allegiance to the star

*actor and refused a monopoly of limelight to the leading
lady. Their art is above petty claims, their aims are beyond
the personal glorification of the individual. Thus they
merit the support of all thinking men and women; their
purpose is firm, and the hope for the future of the drama
lies at the goal they set out to attain: the play is the thing
— Miss Blank or Mister Dash are only the means of
expression to be used when there is something for them to
say.*

The company seems to have put the ensemble approach into
practice, for as an article in *The Times* commented in October:
"the man who has a big part one week is liable to open the door
and announce dinner the next". The programme note concluded
that all that remained was for playgoers to support "the movement which may lead to the establishment of a Scottish National
Theatre".

During the first six weeks of the company's existence Shaw's
You Never Can Tell, Ibsen's *An Enemy of the People*, Galsworthy's *Strife* and Arnold Bennett's *Cupid and Commonsense*,
along with plays by other writers, were produced. The season did
not make a profit and capital was absorbed to cover the operating
loss. The company continued to lose money until the final year
of its existence when it at last made a profit. The figures for the
five years are as follows:

> *1909-1910:* £3,019 loss
> *1910-1911:* £1,539 loss
> *1911-1912:* £322 loss
> *1912-1913:* £125 loss
> *1913-1914:* £790 profit

There is something sadly ironic about the speeches made by
Wareing at the beginning of the enterprise and about some of
the comments in the press. On the first night, 5 April 1909,
Wareing declared "If we go on as we have begun, our 'Citizens'
Theatre' is assured to us". The *Herald* commented seven months
later that a Citizens Theatre had come to stay. Early in 1910 a
proposal was being mooted in the press for a Dramatic Academy
linked to the Repertory Theatre. It was to be forty years before
such a proposal was to be realised, linking a drama college and
a citizens' theatre through the person of their progenitor, James
Bridie.

At the end of the spring season in 1911 Wareing spoke to the audience in the following terms: "If each Repertory enthusiast made a convert, our anxieties would cease and the Repertory Theatre future be assured". The note sounded here had also been sounded in the introductory programme for the season in the autumn of 1910 (on the front cover of which a highlander in warlike garb was shown drawing a curtain). Supporters were exhorted to find new converts in order that the season's programme, which was more costly and ambitious than the previous ones, could be sustained.

In April 1912 Wareing's end of season speech was delivered in his absence, since he had taken ill as a result of overwork. It was not at all optimistic:

This season has been one of ups and downs; there have been many downs, and if the future of the Glasgow Repertory Theatre depended upon the results of this season, I should not feel very happy about it; but hope springs eternal, and I have the courage to think that the results of the next four weeks will revive the ebbing interest. (Glasgow Herald, 29 April 1912)

At that year's AGM at the end of May it was reported that the loss of £322 on the previous thirty-one weeks would have been much higher but for the success of J. J. Bell's *Wee MacGreegor* over the Christmas period. However the directors recommended that a short season be undertaken the following autumn, and extended if successful perhaps by inter-change with other companies involved in the repertory movement.

In addition, Wareing's contract was terminated "in view of the indefiniteness of the future of the company" and it was decided to engage a director on a seasonal basis; although the board indicated that it would be prepared to consider appointing Wareing if he were available in the autumn.

This statement of the directors gave rise to several letters in the Press suggesting ways in which the future of the company could be better secured. Several correspondents suggested that the fourteen hundred seat Royalty Theatre should be abandoned and much smaller and cheaper premises sought. One said that what was required was a small theatre like Gertrude Kingston's Little Theatre in London, which had been opened in 1910 as a repertory theatre, another that a hall seating 400-500 people should be obtained, turned into a workshop theatre with the absolute minimum of equipment, and operated as a private club. The hall could be let in the offseason to bring in extra money. Another suggested that the Repertory Theatre programme had fallen between the two stools of popular and artistic taste, and that high artistic standards were the key to success. Yet another correspondent returned to the old theme of the need to create a Scottish national theatre on the model of the Abbey.

There was no autumn season in 1912, as the directors were unable to obtain a lease of a theatre on favourable terms, although a short programme of plays was presented in the Alhambra, each play being only one part of a variety show which also included, for example, "Willard, the man who grows in full view of the audience". In the spring of 1913 Alfred Wareing, who had been on a cruise to recover his health, returned to Glasgow and presented a short season of plays which included two private performances of Shaw's *Mrs Warren's Profession*, an event which led inevitably to questions being asked in Parliament. Wareing presented this season on his own account. It had no connection with Scottish Playgoers Ltd., which was at the time preoccupied with its doubtful future. Wareing's season, in which he presented nine plays, eight of which were new to Glasgow and four new to the stage, was apparently a financial success, but only just.

Meanwhile a meeting of Scottish Playgoers Ltd. had been called, since several of the large shareholders had indicated that the company might have to consider winding up. However, at the meeting the directors were instructed to carry on, and it was decided to run an eight-week season the following autumn.

The season actually materialised in the spring of 1914 under the directorship of Lewis Casson. Twenty-two plays were presented in thirteen and a half weeks, four of which were new to Glasgow and four new to the stage. The season was the first which was both a financial and an artistic success and the directors were able to report in May 1914 that a profit of over £790 had been made. Colonel F. L. Morrison, the then chairman, remarked at this meeting that he thought they had at last turned the corner and had reached a self-supporting stage. He made the point that the margin of profitability was narrow, since average weekly receipts were only nine pounds higher than two years previously when a loss of £322 had been sustained. It was decided that the name of the company should be changed to the Scottish Repertory Company Ltd. and that a bolder policy would be followed in future, in particular with regard to the production of modern and Shakespearean plays, despite the expense of presenting them. The company had little chance to pursue this bolder policy, for the outbreak of the First World War swamped their efforts. On 16 November 1914 the following paragraph appeared in the Press:

The directors of the Scottish Repertory Company (Ltd.) have decided that owing to the war the active operations of the company must meantime be suspended. Before the outbreak of the war negotiations had been opened with a view to obtaining a suitable theatre, the intention being to enter upon a dramatic season on the lines of the one which proved so successful in the spring of the present year. The war, however, interfered with the arrangements and with Colonel Morrison, Chairman of the company and Major Jowitt, convenor of the production committee, on military service, it was felt that the proposal to proceed with a dramatic season should be postponed and this step has accordingly been taken. Among members of last season's acting company and other members of the staff who are now in France, is the producer, Mr Lewis Casson, who is serving as a motor driver at the front. (Glasgow Herald, 16 November 1914)

The work of the Glasgow Repertory was at an end, and although the remaining funds were transferred after the war to the St. Andrew Society of Glasgow, under whose aegis the Scottish National Players were formed, the nature of the work of the Players was so different from that of the Glasgow Rep. that the tradition started by the latter was not properly restored until the recent growth of professional repertory theatres in Scotland.

It is wrong to look upon the Glasgow Rep. as in any way a failure. Although it had to struggle for the five years of its existence, it had by 1914 reached a reasonably secure position as a serious repertory theatre without benefit of subsidy. Admittedly the company received private subsidy from its shareholders who did not gain, nor expect to gain, any return for their investment, but the fact that a profit was made in 1914 does indicate that a repertory theatre had so established itself in the city that it could have been thenceforth a viable financial proposition. It was the first repertory theatre in Scotland, one of the first in Britain (though it never played strictly in repertoire) and the first citizens' theatre in the English-speaking world. In five years it presented over one hundred plays, thirty-three of which were new to the stage, and some sixteen of which were new Scottish plays. The company performed plays by some of the leading writers of the day — seven by Shaw, two by Ibsen, four by Bennett, three by Galsworthy and three by Granville-Barker. It could not of course be regarded as a thorough going arts or avant-garde theatre, but although lightweight material was presented, the proportion was no higher than that found in the programmes of many subsidised repertory theatres today.

As can be seen from the figures quoted above, one third of all the plays presented were entirely new to the stage, a remarkably high proportion. The company scored a few notable firsts, in particular with the presentation of Chekhov's *The Seagull*, the first production of a play by Chekhov in Britain (Wareing's presentation during his own 1913 season of *Mrs Warren's Profession* was the first production of a censored play outside London). Encouragement was given to Scottish authors, and although no masterpieces were produced and there was no upsurge comparable to the Irish one, a start was made to the building up of a native dramatic tradition. It can be argued that the formation of the Scottish National Players, for all the differing nature of that enterprise, stemmed directly from the encouragement given by the Glasgow Rep. to Scottish writers.

Among the Scots who wrote for the Rep. were Neil Munro, J. J. Bell, G. J. Hamlen, R. K. Risk, Donald Colquhoun, Anthony Rowley and J. A. Ferguson. Harold Chapin, the English writer who had a large number of his plays premiered at the Royalty, tried his hand at Scots drama with *The Philosopher of Butterbiggins*, later performed by the Scottish National Players but never by the Glasgow Rep., in which he captures the Scots idiom fairly successfully but does not put it to any particular purpose.

G. J. Hamlen, a chemist at Nobel's plant in Stevenston, had several of his plays performed at the Royalty — *Barbara Grows Up*, *The Truth About De Courcy* (with Alfred Wareing), *How Cottle Fell from Grace*, *Colin in Fairyland* (a pantomime) and *The Waldies* (this last during Wareing's own 1913 season). They are well-made plays but forgettable, although *Barbara Grows Up* (6 September 1909, Royalty) does toy with several important social questions, without really exploring them.

Anthony Rowley is a very similar kind of writer to Hamlen. The Repertory Company produced two of his plays — *A Weaver's Shuttle* and *The Probationer*. *A Weaver's Suttle* (21 November 1910, Royalty) is set in Robbiesburgh, West Lothian, and deals with a family firm in difficulties. It is a play which is theatrically effective but of no depth. One thing to be said in its favour, however, is that it is about the life of the lowland Scottish middle class and, although it is a superficial play, it does seek to mirror the life of its time in an honest fashion. The same point can be made about *The Probationer*, which is also set in Robbiesburgh and the nearby city of Edinburgh.

John Joy Bell, the prolific author of *Wee MacGreegor*, had several plays presented by the Glasgow Rep. — *Wee MacGreegor* itself, *The Best Man*, *Providing for Marjorie* and *Oh Christina*.

The two best Scottish plays produced by the Glasgow Rep. were Donald Colquhoun's *Jean* (of which Wareing thought very highly) and J. A. Ferguson's *Campbell of Kilmohr*, which was presented during the season under the directorship of Lewis Casson, and has been much revived since, particularly in the amateur theatre.

Jean (16 May 1910, Royalty) is set in a farmhouse in Lanarkshire, and despite a rather melodramatic plot has the great merit of honesty in its presentation of the hard life of the small farmer as he tries to establish himself in a position of security. The remarks Milroy, an old farmer, makes to his son about his dead wife ring true:

JAMES   Afore ye kent yer mither an' me, we wis by wi'
     the worst o't, we wis kinna weel aff, and easy like . . .
     But ye should have seen us when we started. Man, it was
     a fair wrastle, day an' nicht — nicht an' day. I widna
     like ye to hiv yon tae dae.
SANDY   It couldna be as bad for me — noo.
JAMES   Mind ye, it's no' every woman wad hiv turned
     oot like yer mither. She got on rael weel. There was a
     wheen years there, afore she deed, ye widna hiv kenned
     her for the same woman — she wis that sensible and
     wise — like. But there's no' mony lassies turns oot like
     her. The maist o' them gangs intae their graves wi' nae

> mair sense in their heids than the first day they stairted
> courtin'. Na, na, Sandy, dinna think o't yet. Ye ken fine
> I'm layin' by for ye. Ye'll be fit to staun' in wi' the best
> o' them.

As can be seen, the Scots dialogue is effective without being quaint. The play itself follows the course of an argument between the old farmer and his son Sandy over the question of Sandy's marriage to the farm maid — Jean of the title. The argument ends on a dramatic note with the revelation by Milroy that Jean has previously had an illegitimate child, the counter-revelation by Sandy that he has already married Jean, and the consequent fatal seizure that kills Milroy.

Campbell of Kilmohr (23 March 1914, Royalty) is set in the Highlands after the '45 and in it Ferguson is concerned to contrast the integrity of the Highlander with the dishonesty and roguery of the Lowlander. It is a new experience for Campbell, a Lowlander and Government official, to find that his wiles in seeking to prise information about the Pretender's whereabouts from Highlanders are unsuccessful. His ideas on human nature up to this point in time have been straightforward:

> Now, I've had a lairge experience o' life, and I never saw
> yet a sensible man insensible to the touch of yellow metal.
> If there may be such a man, it is demonstrable that he is
> no sensible man. Fideelity! quotha, it's sheer obstinacy.
> They just see that he wants something oot o' them, and
> they're so damned selfish and thrawn they winna pairt.
> And with the natural inabeelity o' their brains to hold mair
> than one idea at a time they canna see that in return you
> could put something into their palms far more profitable.

Campbell, however, is forced to change his ideas in the face of Highland obstinacy and to resort to the trickery of a young girl in an attempt to secure the information he requires. Having gained the information he wants, he cynically goes back on an undertaking not to execute Morag's cousin Dugald. The final irony is that what he has been told about the Jacobites is misleading and he is no further forward in his hunt for them.

Campbell of Kilmohr is a slight play but its merit is that it is true to life, though as a reading of *The Lyon in Mourning* or a viewing of Peter Watkins' film *Culloden* make clear, the events of 1746 had a barbarity scarcely hinted at by Ferguson. It is, however, a dramatically effective piece and does not lean too heavily on cliche ideas about the Highlands.

It may seem disappointing that these two are the only plays among all those presented by the Glasgow Repertory Company which in any meaningful way reflect the life and history of Scotland. But it is better to have two plays than none.

Another effect on the development of Scottish drama traceable to the Glasgow Repertory Company is more difficult to measure. The existence of a theatre presenting new Scottish plays may well have encouraged potential dramatists to write for the stage and thus to begin learning their craft. We do know, for example, that the young Bridie was encouraged by what he saw at the Royalty to try his hand, and indeed he actually submitted a play to Wareing, although it was never performed.

Turning now to the reasons for the Glasgow Rep's demise, in the first place the point must be made that it was a pioneer in its field and pioneering is a hazardous activity. To have been able in five years to make a profit from one season was a significant achievement — after all five years is a very short time in which to create an audience for non-commercial theatre. That audiences at the Royalty were at times very thin indeed was attested by James Bridie forty years later:

> *The other day I happened to see the accounts of the first two years of the Glasgow Repertory and was once more astounded by the number of bricks Wareing was able to make out of the few wisps of straw that the wind blew into his playhouse. On one occasion he opened to an audience of five schoolmistresses in the pit. He came in front of the curtain and invited them to the front row of the stalls. The performance was then given and the actors never enjoyed themselves so much in their lives.* (Foreword to *Alfred Wareing*, W. Isaac, London 1951)

We might be forgiven for doubting the last statement.

During the course of a talk which he gave in London in 1912, Wareing , having praised Glasgow's sense of civic solidarity, admitted that grey towns did not make for good dramatic art. He then rather frivolously expressed the hope that a populace that could drill itself into dropping used tram tickets in boxes could surely do the equally improbable and support a repertory theatre.

As has been previously indicated, some of the people who wrote letters to the papers in 1912, when there was doubt as to whether the Rep. would continue, suggested that the company should be less ambitious, hire a small hall, use the very minimum of equipment and cater only for the small minority of theatre lovers in the city. This, no doubt, could have been done, but it would have been contrary to the whole spirit of the scheme, which was to create a popular audience for serious theatre. The converted can be induced into bare, ill-heated halls, but if the aim is to attract the unconverted, the facilities of a fully-equipped theatre, on and off stage, are essential.

Another correspondent suggested that the board of directors, competent business men though they might be, knew nothing of the theatre. This is an uncharitable view: most voluntary committees know little professionally of the organisation they are serving and it is for that reason that they hire professionals, as Scottish Playgoers Ltd. hired Wareing and after him Lewis Casson.

The inevitable criticism that the company did not produce enough Scottish material was made. There was, as has been indicated, a fair amount of Scottish material presented, but little of it was of a particularly high standard and one suspects that a programme made up entirely of Scottish plays would have been very dismal indeed. There is nothing to be gained from setting up a repertory theatre which aims at international standards in choice of play and production, and then flings these standards completely overboard when it comes to dealing with local plays. True, a theatre is bound to be less demanding if it wishes to encourage the development of local talent, but it is in the interest of Scottish drama that it competes with the drama of other nations under roughly the same rules.

It is interesting, if ironic, to set alongside the complaint that the Glasgow Rep. did not perform enough Scottish drama this judgement made by *The Times*:

> *There is no great enthusiasm in Glasgow about a Scottish Theatre; Glasgow men prefer to see English plays. Scotch writers are too sentimental for the Scotch: they have to go to London.*

As of course did Barrie. Other writers, however, stayed in Scotland and attention will now be turned in their direction.

CHAPTER FOUR

Between the Wars — The Curtain and Robert McLellan

THE INTER-WAR PERIOD IN SCOTLAND was the period of the so-called Scottish Renaissance, a rejuvenation in Scottish literature which took place against the background of a growing but ultimately ineffective campaign for home rule, in contrast to the situation in the seventies where a similar political campaign may produce substantial devolution of power to Scotland at a time when Scottish writing has appeared to be suffering from a serious crisis of identity and direction. The crisis appears to be in the process of being resolved now, particularly as far as the drama is concerned, but it is interesting to note the present time lag between the growth rates of political and cultural nationalism — indeed the lack of formal contacts between the two, compared to the situation between the wars when the interaction was substantial.

To return to the inter-war period, it would be as well to relate theatrical developments to the renaissance as a whole. In August 1922 the first number of C. M. Grieve's *Scottish Chapbook* appeared and in it was printed 'The Chapbook Programme' which can be taken as an idiosyncratic presentation of the aims of the renaissance. The Programme gives an important place to the theatre, but the principal aims and objects of the Scottish Chapbook are:

> *To report, support and stimulate, in particular, the activities of the Franco-Scottish, Scottish-Italian, and kindred Associations; the campaign of the Vernacular Circle of the London Burns Club for the revival of the Doric; the movement towards a Scots National Theatre; and the 'Northern Numbers' movement in contemporary Scottish poetry. To encourage and publish the work of contemporary Scottish poets and dramatists, whether in English, Gaelic, or Braid Scots. To insist upon truer evaluations of the work of Scottish writers than are usually given in the present over-Anglicised condition of British literary journalism, and, in criticism, elucidate, apply, and*

develop the distinctively Scottish range of values.
To bring Scottish Literature into closer touch with current
European tendencies in technique and ideation.
To cultivate 'the lovely virtue'.
And generally, to 'meddle wi' the Thistle' and pick the
figs.

Grieve's contribution to the renaissance movement in his own person as propagandist and critic, and as his alter ego, poet Hugh MacDiarmid, was of the first importance, as was Neil Gunn's in the field of the novel. As far as drama is concerned, the magazines Grieve edited, such as *The Northern Review*, give a fair proportion of space to original plays, to articles on the theatre, and to dramatic criticism. The other literary and general magazines of the period, as will be seen from what follows, also gave generously of their space to the discussion of the Scottish theatre and the publication of plays.

The resurgence in Scottish literature took place against a background of two major cultural developments that were and still are making a world impact: cinema and broadcasting. Cinemas began to appear in Scotland in the early years of the twentieth century, often in makeshift premises. Their number climbed steadily after the First World War, as can be seen from the following figures:

NUMBER OF CINEMAS IN SCOTLAND

	Total	Aberdeen	Dundee	Edinburgh	Glasgow
1920	557	15	22	25	94
1930	634	15	27	39	127
1940	615	19	25	38	112

Obviously a vast popular audience had come into existence and grown at a remarkable rate, for whereas in 1920 there were over five hundred cinemas twenty years previously there were no institutions that would be recognised as such.

Regular broadcasting came to Scotland in 1923 when the British Broadcasting Company's Glasgow station was opened; other stations at Edinburgh and Aberdeen followed and the growth in the number of licence holders was substantial throughout the inter-war period. Early on the BBC in Scotland began to broadcast drama: an adaptation of *Rob Roy* was mounted a few weeks after the Glasgow station opened; and in 1932 the Scottish service mounted its first Radio Drama Festival.

The consequences of these two developments — cinema and broadcasting — were many. As far as theatre is concerned, the rapid decline of the music hall, which had enjoyed a boom before the war, can be attributed to their growth. Many music halls and variety theatres became cinemas: for example, Glasgow's Britannia, later the Panopticon, became the Tron Cinema in 1920; the Savoy opened in the same city in 1911 as a variety theatre and was a cinema by 1916. In Dundee the Palace was a cinema by 1911 (though during the Second World War it reverted to variety). In Edinburgh the Grand became a cinema in 1920. Elsewhere in Scotland theatres were converted: Greenock's Alexandra in the mid-twenties, Kirkcaldy's King's in 1924, Falkirk's Grand in 1934.

The extent to which the theatrical expansion in the first decade of the century had been halted and reversed can be seen by looking at the relevant figures:

NUMBER OF THEATRES IN SCOTLAND

	Total	Aberdeen	Dundee	Edinburgh	Glasgow
1920	45	3	3	6	16
1930	30	3	0	4	12
1940	32	3	1	6	11

The decline from the 1910 position was most marked, among the cities, in Dundee and Glasgow. Elsewhere in Scotland there was a steady slide, so that by 1940 there were over a third less theatres in Scotland than there had been in 1910.

While cinema provided little extra employment for Scottish writers and actors, radio began to open up some new opportunities, but neither development had quite as dramatic an effect on live theatre as television in its turn was to have later on the cinema. Theatre survived but remained a minority interest, for the mass audience did not support it. Whereas previously that audience had patronised the music hall, now vastly increased in numbers by reason of higher incomes, it gave its allegiance to the cinema and the wireless, an allegiance later transferred to television. Professional theatre it passed by completely.

In Scotland the professional theatre was represented as before by touring companies and a small number of repertory companies based north of the border. These companies co-operated closely with the theatrical management of Howard and Wyndham, the Edinburgh company formed in 1895 with two of the leading theatrical figures of the day, J. B. Howard and F. W. Wyndham, as joint managing directors. Many performances were given in two of the company's premier theatres — the Edinburgh Lyceum and the Theatre Royal in Glasgow. It is a reflection of the present that Howard and Wyndham have sold these theatres and many others over the last few years. They now derive only 6 per cent of turnover (1976 figures) from their theatre operations, whereas in 1970 the figure was 70 per cent. Publishing and book distribution now account for most of their trading, and the company is continuing a policy of "minimising exposure to the caprices of theatre ownership" — to quote the words of their chairman.

The first of the repertory companies to establish itself in this period was the Masque Theatre, which was founded in 1928 under Robert Fenemore and alternated between Glasgow and Edinburgh for the next five years. In late 1932 a plan for the establishment of a permanent repertory theatre building in Edinburgh was announced, but it never came to anything and the company effectively ceased to exist. Its place on the Howard and Wyndham circuit was taken by the Brandon-Thomas Players, a company which had been formed in 1930 and had given its first performance in Newcastle. Thereafter it had toured throughout Britain and came north to Edinburgh for a fourteen-week season in 1933. This season and a subsequent one in Glasgow were deemed so successful that the company stayed in Scotland until, in 1937, it decided to try its fortune in London. Sad to say the transfer to the capital was not a success and the company was disbanded early in 1938. It is interesting to note however that among the actors was Wilson Barrett whose own repertory company was established shortly after the Brandon-Thomas one disappeared. That company was to come north permanently in 1941 and to provide regular repertory seasons until 1955. In 1938 Howard and Wyndham filled the gap left by the departure of the Brandon-Thomas Players by sponsoring a repertory company of its own which performed until the outbreak of war in 1939.

Collectively all the ventures described above were a forerunner of the modern repertory theatres, of which we now have a fair number in Scotland. They were, of course, a retreat from the position of the Glasgow Repertory Company and their programming was less adventurous, but they did keep professional theatre alive in Scotland and continued the important work of audience-building: the Brandon-Thomas Players claimed patronage latterly of ten thousand persons per week in each of the two theatres in which they performed, although they had had a lean period during the very worst years of the Depression. Scottish drama did find a place in their programmes: Bridie's *The Anatomist* was given its premiere by the Masque Theatre. However the Scottish element in the repertoires of these companies was not a large one.

London-originated tours still occupied many stages in Scotland for much of the time. These took the form of plays, musicals and variety shows. The First World War had shown the popularity of musical comedy — *Chu Chin Chow* opened in London in 1916 and ran for over two thousand performances — and this continued after the war. Variety shows were a smoother, more cosmetic form of entertainment than the old music hall and more respectable, of course; but something of the music hall survived north of the border in the work of Scots comedians like Harry Gordon, Tommy Lorne, Tommy Morgan and Dave Willis in both variety and pantomime.

A repertory theatre about which more will be said later was established in Perth in 1935, but persistent attempts to found a professional theatre in Edinburgh were unsuccessful, as were efforts to establish a municipal theatre in Glasgow and a Scottish national theatre towards the end of the thirties. It was only when the Edinburgh Gateway and Glasgow Citizens' theatres opened in 1946 and 1943 respectively that these cities gained permanent repertory theatres. The various little theatres which were established — at Dundee and St. Andrews for example — were for the use of amateurs. The Curtain Theatre in Glasgow presented its work in a large room in a West End mansion which had a capacity of sixty-five. The Glasgow Jewish Institute Players opened a theatre in their Institute in 1938.

The development of drama during this period was largely in the hands of such amateur clubs who thrived between the wars rather than in those of the professional theatre. Members of the companies at the forefront of the renaissance, the Scottish National Players and the Curtain, normally received no payment for their work, apart from fees for radio broadcasts, but nonetheless found themselves charged with the responsibility of creating a national drama.

The amateur theatre movement in Britain, as we now know it, began in the middle of the nineteenth century as essentially a pursuit of the upper and middle classes, and by the turn of the century was firmly established. By the end of the First World War it was such a significant activity among all social classes that there came into being associations of amateur clubs, the British Drama League being founded in 1919, and the Scottish Community Drama Association in 1926, the latter with the aims of encouraging the drama in Scotland and organising festivals of community drama. The sudden rise to popularity of the amateur theatre in Scotland can be seen by comparing the number of entries for the one-act festival in 1926-27 (35), 1928-29 (88) and 1930-31 (243); by the 1932-33 season the entry had reached 307. By 1937 there were more than one thousand amateur clubs in Scotland.

It is difficult for people who did not live through the boom period in amateur drama to realize how extensive the activity was. A perusal of the newspapers of the time makes it clear that this was no coterie pursuit but one in which a lot of people were either involved or interested. The Scottish newspapers of the thirties, for example, all had regular weekly columns on the amateur scene and reviews of productions. The development of the play festivals, whatever it may have done for standards — and this is a matter very much open to debate — certainly appears to have aroused public interest. Apparently the fortunes of one particular group who had success on a national and international scale, the Ardrossan and Saltcoats Players, were followed locally like those of a football team.

The amateur theatre movement seems to have grown in part out of the Victorian impulse towards self-improvement and from the initially domestic evenings of entertainment which they provided for one another. The upsurge in the twentieth century can be attributed to the general increase in leisure time, the expansion of education and the realisation, particularly in areas relatively far from large centres of population with professional theatres, that in this activity not only was there the opportunity for large-scale community involvement but also a clear way of participating and gaining access to the arts. After a certain point was reached, of course, amateur drama had become a fashion if not a craze, and it was inevitable that when some other fashion came along the less dedicated clubs would die, as in fact has happened since the advent of television. In 1951 the SCDA's one-act festival could still attract five hundred entries, but by the early sixties the number had halved.

What was the effect of all this activity on the growth of the Scottish theatre? William Power, the journalist who wrote frequently on the drama at the time, expressed the opinion that the SCDA (and the Scottish National Players) were perhaps winning people over to good plays. However, it has to be said he is almost alone in taking this view. Joe Corrie, the playwright, remarked that 75% of amateur groups

> *are not interested in drama as an art so much as they are interested in it as an amusement. Their primary object is to make their audience laugh, a process which they themselves enjoy.* (SMT Magazine, November 1937)

An extremely outspoken attack on the community drama movement was made by another writer, Clyde Irvine. In an article entitled *Drama for Dumb Bells* he rejected the oft-vaunted contention that there was a resemblance between the Scottish amateur drama movement and the Abbey Theatre. As far as the plays presented by amateur clubs were concerned,

> *These "sappy" plays are written by people who believe that the average Scots audience is composed of dumb bells . . . we are content to see season after season the amateur stage of Scotland made a penny geggie for the perpetuation of as crass and ignorant a policy as ever disgraced any national attempt at self-expression.* (The Scots Magazine, March 1938)

Although these comments are excessively critical and may contain an element of sour grapes, it has to be admitted there is some substance in them. As anyone who has had any dealings with the amateur drama movement in Scotland will confirm, the self-expression of the Scottish nation through the drama is not always very high on its list of objectives. Some amateurs are not even particularly interested in the theatre. Most enjoy the experience of acting and make an important contribution to the life of their communities, but would not consider that the creation of a Scottish drama was a fundamental part of their activities. That is not to say that they take no interest in Scottish plays, but their interest is often rather parochial and un-adventurous.

This situation seems to have been a major factor in preventing the growth of a Scottish drama totally worthy of respect between the wars. We must remember that the amateur drama movement, apart from the Scottish National Players, who occupied a special position, was well nigh the only outlet for Scottish writers in their own country. The role of the Players in this situation, with their declared aim of promoting exclusively Scottish drama, was therefore very important. The initiative in founding the Scottish Community Drama Association actually came from the Players. D. Glen Mackemmie, their secretary, was approached by the British Drama League in London seeking to involve Scottish amateur clubs in a competitive festival. The winning team was to visit the USA to compete for the David Belasco Cup against American drama clubs. A meeting of British Drama League clubs in Scotland was called and the SCDA established. The links between the Scottish National Players and the SCDA were clearly seen when Mackemmie was appointed vice-chairman. It is interesting to note that two years later in 1928 the Ardrossan and Saltcoats Players won their way to the American festival and carried off the Belasco Trophy with their production of Barrie's *The Old Lady Shows Her Medals*.

Before considering the Scottish National Players, to which separate chapters will be devoted, more detailed mention must be made of some of the other theatrical ventures of this period. Two of these, the repertory theatres at Dundee and Rutherglen, began operations respectively after and just before the Second World War started. They will therefore be dealt with more appropriately in the chapter concerned with the Scottish theatre during the war.

Perth Repertory Theatre was a joint venture by Marjorie Dence and David Steuart, who had met at London University where they were both studying. Steuart's ambition of starting a rep. in Perth was realised when a theatre was advertised for sale in the city. Perth's first regular theatre had opened in 1810 and although it was destroyed by fire in 1824 another theatre, the Royal, which had opened in 1820 continued to operate until mid-century. Perth Theatre opened in 1900 and housed a variety of travelling companies until it was put up for sale by its owner. Marjorie Dence's father now assisted in the theatre's acquistion and it opened again on 23 September 1935 with a production of Clifford Bax's *Rose without a Thorn*. By 1939 it felt secure enough to organise a theatre festival, for which Bridie wrote *The Golden Legend of Shults* and at which performances of *Romeo and Juliet* (with Alec Guinness), Chekhov's *Three Sisters* and Shaw's *Caesar and Cleopatra* were also given.

The Curtain was started by a group of amateur enthusiasts led by Grace Ballantine who, with a mere £100 in capital, hired a large L-shaped drawing room in a house in Glasgow's Woodside Terrace and turned it into an auditorium with seating for sixty-five people. The aim was to provide a stage where the practising playwright might see his work being rehearsed or performed and this was done initially from January 1933 in the tiny Curtain Theatre itself and from 1935-1940 in the Lyric Theatre, formerly the Royalty. To begin with about six programmes a year were given and the audience was made up of subscribers. The Curtain was an amateur club very different in kind from the typical club that was criticised so vehemently by playwrights in the thirties.

Of the actors who worked with the Curtain, Molly Urquhart, who later founded the Rutherglen Repertory Theatre and then joined the Citizens' Company, and Duncan Macrae are best known. Macrae learnt his craft with the Curtain, attracting much attention for his performances, particularly for his creation of the title role in Robert McLellan's *Jamie the Saxt*. He was born in 1905, the son of a Sutherland crofter who had, like many of his fellow Highlanders, emigrated southwards to Glasgow and joined the police force. After studying engineering at Glasgow University Macrae took up school teaching and acted in his spare time. He was later to join the Citizens' company on its inception in 1943 and after a few years with it to exploit his marvellous and grotesque comic talent in pantomime as well as in the straight theatre. He was the most talented Scottish actor to emerge from the amateur movement and his death in 1967 was a great loss to the theatre and also television. The musical adviser to the Curtain, John Stewart, later opened the Park Theatre (next door to the Curtain) and, when it closed, the Pitlochry Festival Theatre, which will be discussed in a later chapter.

Although the aim was to encourage Scottish plays, the Curtain had difficulty in attracting enough worthwhile native material and in making it commercially viable. Despite this problem, its record of encouraging Scottish writers deserves credit. Among the writers whose work was performed at the Curtain were George Malcolm Thompson (in whose *A Letter to Rome* Macrae played Cardinal Beaton), Robins Millar, Norman Bruce (one of the people most involved in running the company), Paul Vincent Carroll and above all, Robert McLellan, the most significant exponent of Lallans plays.

Before discussing McLellan, it is worth saying a little in passing about Carroll's best-known play *Green Cars Go East*, which was premiered not by the Curtain but by The Glasgow Players (30 November 1937, Lyric). Set against the background of Glasgow's East End it centres on the efforts of Mary Lewis, a young schoolteacher who has raised herself above her background and parents — a drunken unemployed father and ineffectual mother — to keep the family out of trouble with the law and to ensure that her two brothers also escape from their sordid circumstances. Her efforts are, in the end, successful. The play is a good example of urban naturalism, although the characterisation is at times on the weak side and the author does not make much of a connection between character and environment, but it has the substantial merit of representing an important aspect of the life of Scotland on the stage.

Although Robert McLellan has written much since the demise of the Curtain it would be as well to consider his work as a whole at this point when the theatre, where his earliest plays were performed, is being discussed.

McLellan, who was born in 1907 and has supported himself by his writing for most of his life, grew up partly on a farm where he heard Scots dialect used and spoken until he was a young man. The Scots he uses in his plays is based on spoken language and is not a synthetic construct. After the controversy which arose out of MacDiarmid's use of Jamieson's dictionary to cull words with which the poet himself was not familiar, McLellan resolved that he, as a playwright, would never resort to this device. In fact, he has said that he has found himself on occasion using words which cannot be found in Jamieson, but which he is nonetheless sure he has heard used in the past.

That he has a fine grasp of Scots is the first thing that strikes one about McLellan's work. The dialogue moves vigorously and naturally; it is a living language that is being spoken, not some anachronistic artifact — as this extract from *Toom Byres* makes clear:

SIR ROBERT   Weill, I propose, Sir Andra, to let ye keep
the stock ye hae liftit frae the Hanginshaw, for I
conseeder ye less to blame for tha affair nor Wat here.

WAT   Eh!

SIR ROBERT   Juist haud yer tongue the noo, sir! I was
sayin, Sir Andra, that I propose to let ye keep the stock
ye hae liftit frae the Hanginshaw, and I hae entert a
clause in the bond to that effect. Ye may regaird it as a
jeynt tocher o the two Hanginshaw lassies, wha are to
mairry yer sons.

WAT   Hae my byres and stables to bide toom?

SIR ROBERT   Sir Andra will doubtless let ye hae yer
stock back gin ye mak him a guid offer in ready siller.

WAT   And had there to be one tocher wi his dochter?

SIR ROBERT   I hae made nae proveesion in the bond for
ony sic thing.

On the other hand, McLellan, who recalls with great regret
that every time he wrote a successful play in Scots he was
encouraged from all sides to write in English, does not have the
same facility with that language. Using it, he produces dialogue
that is often limp and lifeless, quite lacking the theatricality of
his Scots, something for which only part of the blame can be put
on the state of the English language itself.

McLellan's plays are almost all set in the past, in eighteenth-
century Edinburgh, in the Borders of the early seventeenth
century, at the courts of Mary Queen of Scots or James the
Sixth. He prefers to write about the past because he feels that in
writing about the present day the dramatist is liable to become
so bogged down in its trivia that his work dates very quickly,
whereas if plays are set in a historical period, the dramatist is
freed from the deadening weight of such details. It is a tenable,
if limiting, view of the relationship between a writer and his
society.

McLellan's view of history contrasts sharply with that of
many other Scottish writers. Whereas they often regard the
events of the past through romantic spectacles, McLellan
presents a more believable and harsher world, even although he
is writing comedy. Rather sudden death comes uncomfortably
close to Archie Armstrong in *The Changeling* when he steals one
of the Elliots' sheep, and to Will Scott in *Jeddart Justice* when

he refuses to marry one of Sir Gideon Murray's daughters as recompense for a similar misdeed. The laird of *Torwatletie* inhabits a world of unattractive scheming rascals. James Boswell is presented in *Young Auchinleck* without any attempt to hide his excesses or the venereal disease which ensued in consequence. Samuel Skinner in *The Hypocrite* is a bigot, supported by legions of other bigots. *Jamie the Saxt* finds himself in the midst of intriguing lords and only survives by consummate deviousness, while the Arran of *The Cailleach* and *The Smuggler* is one where violent death can leave a girl to bear an illegitimate child or a young smuggler can be forced to flee his native country for ever to escape the gaugers.

This aspect of McLellan's work must in fairness be emphasised — given the strong trendency running through Scottish culture to sentimentalise the past. Nonetheless one feels disappointment that McLellan has never felt able to tackle large contemporary themes. *The Road to the Isles* (22 February 1954, Citizens'), set on a Scottish island in recent times, attempts to deal with such a theme, namely the regeneration of the Highlands; but unfortunately the play's energies are dissipated as McLellan tilts at a variety of irrelevant windmills. Only two of his historical plays could be related to the contemporary world — *The Hypocrite* and *The Flouers o Edinburgh*.

The Hypocrite (3 August 1967, Royal Lyceum) is set in eighteenth-century Edinburgh and centres on the activities of a minister, Samuel Skinner, who successfully prevents an exhibition of Italian engravings from being shown in several Scottish cities on the grounds that they are obscene. Skinner is shown to be a lascivious hypocrite whose obsession with nakedness is far from innocent, a man who will happily sleep with a married woman to advance his son's career. Skinner is surrounded by clergymen and burghers as bigoted as himself, and McLellan obviously intends the play as a satirical comment on the civic reaction to the Edinburgh Festival 'happening' in 1963. This happening was staged on the last day of a rather unexciting drama conference and served both as a comment on the conference and as a way of livening up speakers and audience. It was amusing and inventive, but part of it consisted of a nude girl being pulled momentarily across the balcony above the speakers' platform.

The papers the next day (appropriately, perhaps, Sunday)

headlined the NUDE AT FESTIVAL and did not, of course, bother to relate the appearance of the nude girl to the context. The Lord Provost made an inane statement, lamenting the fact that "three weeks of glorious festival should have been smeared by a piece of pointless vulgarity", and refusing to surrender "to the irresponsible actions of a few people sick in heart and mind". The model who had participated in the happening was summoned on an indecency charge of which she was later acquitted. In *The Hypocrite*, historically placed beyond libel action, McLellan renders the reactions to the drama conference events ridiculous, and suggests that they are not as innocent as they might appear.

The Flouers o Edinburgh (13 September 1948, Glasgow Unity in King's, Edinburgh) — again set in eighteenth-century Edinburgh — has as its main theme the conflict of mind felt by the gentry of that time as to whether they should speak Scots or English, and McLellan has a great deal of fun at the expense of one of his characters who has abandoned his 'barbarous' native tongue. The play can be taken as a comment on the discussion of the use of Scots today. We can deduce that McLellan is in favour of using Scots in literature and perhaps even, it is implied, in daily life.

Apart however from these three plays, there are no substantial themes in McLellan's work. He says in fact that in most of his plays he has been more interested in character than in theme. The characters of historical personages, for example, interest him for their own sake. He is also concerned to present in his plays characters he has known in his own life as a way of 'fixing' certain components of Scottishness which he feels have been ignored by Scottish dramatists. The characters and the conflicts they engender he believes to be endemic in Scotland and still to be encountered today.

Toom Byres (1 May 1936, Curtain Theatre in Lyric, Glasgow), for example, is set in the Borders at Kinnelknock in the early years of the reign of James the Sixth. It concerns the novel method by which Sir Robert o' the Drumford, Keeper of the Dale, resolves a quarrel between the Kers and the Scotts by pairing off the young members of the families in marriage. The play is much more involved than this bare summary would suggest and McLellan handles the complexities of the plot well. The characters, particularly Wat Scott of the Hanginshaw and

Peggy Ker, are strong, well-defined, recognisably Scottish creations.

The Changeling and *Jeddart Justice* (8 January 1934, Curtain) have both already been mentioned and little more need be said of them other than they are amusing, if slight, one-act comedies set in the same milieu as *Toom Byres*.

Three of McLellan's plays are set in the Edinburgh of the eighteenth century, the Edinburgh of Hume and Boswell. *The Flouers o' Edinburgh*, whose relationship to the contemporary scene has been discussed above, reflects the growth of industrialisation and the spread of Anglicisation, two developments which McLellan considers to be very closely linked. The link is to be seen in Charlie Stanebyres who is promoting (in an underhand fashion) industrial development, and insists on speaking in the English manner, going so far as to refuse to marry a girl since she is unwilling to follow suit. The plan for industrialisation is foiled and McLellan extracts much humour at the expense of Charlie and those who join his attempt to emulate the English. The play is amusing and diverting, if not very substantial. The characterisation is on the whole convincing, although one or two characters, introduced it would seem as pawns in the linguistic argument, approach caricature.

Young Auchinleck (20 August 1962, Gateway as part of the Edinburgh Festival) was written out of the author's interest in the conflict between James Boswell and his father Lord Auchinleck. Boswell, McLellan feels, suffered from a repressive Scots upbringing which was directly responsible for the dissolute life that he led as a young man. Lord Auchinleck represents that background against which Boswell is reacting and at one point in the play the conflict becomes so intense that Boswell has difficulty restraining himself from murdering his father. Although the character of Boswell develops from being a rather repulsive rake to a reformed one saved by the love of his cousin Peggy Montgomerie, whom he marries, he is for much of the time a rather boring individual. Lord Auchinleck, speaking a vigorous Scots unlike Boswell who speaks Anglified Scots, is much more interesting than his son, which is unfortunate as Boswell is the central character of the play. This happens quite simply because McLellan writes with far more life in Scots than he does in English.

Mention has already been made of *The Hypocrite* which,

although a comedy, is a very pessimistic account of Scots
puritanism. Skinner's hypocrisy almost catches up with him at
the end of the play, but he avoids disaster and declares himself
saved to carry on with the work of the Lord. The relevance of the
play to contemporary Scotland has been referred to and it does
make an effective point which needs to be made. However, the
play gives the impression of being inflated beyond its proper
dimensions and might have been more effective in one act. As
we might expect, Skinner, who speaks English, often sounds
stilted whereas the few characters who speak Scots come alive
immediately.

McLellan's best play *Jamie the Saxt* (31 March 1937, Curtain
Theatre in Lyric) is notable mainly for the strength of its
characterization. It is set during the period 1591-94 when
the young king was struggling to assert himself at the centre of a
web of conspiracy woven by dissident lords, the Church, the
burghers of Edinburgh and the English Government. It is not a
play which 'says' anything, but the picture of James as a much-
tried young man who survives not by a display of heroics but by
using his wits to play one faction off against another is very
appealing. McLellan's Jamie is not a clown but a canny
individual whose qualities see him through till the end of the
play, when he is able to look forward confidently to claiming the
throne of England:

THE KING: . . . Oho, but fortune's favoured me the day!
There's naething in my wey! Aa that I hae wished for is
promised at last; Bothwell on the scaffold, the Papists
houndit doun, the kirk is my pouer, England ahint me,
and then, in the end the dream o my life come true! It
gars my pulse quicken! It gars my hairt loup! It gars my
een fill wi' tears! To think hou the two puir countries
hae focht and struggled. To think o the bluid they hae
shed atween them, the touns they hae blackent wi fire,
the bonnie green howes they hae laid waste. And then to
think, as ae day it sall come to pass that I, Jamie
Stewart, will ride to London and the two countries sall
become ane. (*Mistress Edward can be heard off calling
'Nicoll! Nicoll! Come for yer supper!'*)

MAITLAND: (*Coming out of his trance and reaching for
the bottle*) Ay, yer Grace, it's a solemn thocht. But the
auld bitch isna deid yet. (*He places the bottle before the*

King. The King fills his glass).

THE KING: (*Raising his glass high*) Jock, here's to the
day. May the mowdies sune tickle her taes.
(*Mistress Edward appears at the door of the dining
room*)

MISTRESS EDWARD: Yer Grace, the supper's ready.
(*The King and Maitland eye each other and drink the
toast*)

The play, when originally performed, served as a vehicle for
a highly individual performance by Duncan Macrae, although
McLellan does not appear to have been in complete agreement
with Macrae's interpretation of the character which rather
prophetically revealed the gift for pantomime that Macrae was
later to exploit.

A characteristic which *Jamie the Saxt* shares with *Torwatletie* (18 November 1946, Unity in Queen's Theatre, Glasgow) is
the intricate, not to say confusing, plot structure which McLellan
obviously enjoys creating. *Torwatletie* is set near the Solway in
1716. The Laird of Torwatletie, mainly to spite the Calvinist
Presbyterians typified by his sister Mirren, harbours a Jacobite
refugee who is to be helped to escape to the Isle of Man. This is
accomplished after much scheming and counter-scheming
involving a displaced Episcopalian curate, a Presbyterian spy
and a local rascal who is engaged in smuggling and press-
ganging. It is a lively piece of theatre which relies over-heavily at
times on horseplay, but is not of any great account. McLellan's
dislike of Calvinism is again in evidence, but it is not developed
as a theme.

To conclude, Robert McLellan is a playwright who has
indeed demonstrated considerable theatrical talent and skill;
nonetheless it can only be a matter of regret that so far he has
been unable to find very many important themes attractive
enough to engage that talent and skill. Perhaps the problem has
been a linguistic one. At ease with a language which, although not
archaic, contains words and idioms which would not be familiar
to modern urban Scots, McLellan probably could write plays
of the kind we have seen more recently in the Scottish theatre for
linguistic reasons alone. For all the vivacity of his Scots dialogue,
McLellan's language is ultimately an insuperable barrier between
himself and the modern world and indeed a defence against that
world.

CHAPTER FIVE

The Scottish National Players — The Company and the Major Dramatists

THE SCHEME FOR THE FORMATION of the Scottish National players was initiated before the First World War under the auspices of the St. Andrew Society of Glasgow and was aimed at the "production of plays dealing with Scottish life and character". The War, however, led to its postponement, although attempts were made during the hostilities to foster interest by arranging a series of lectures and meetings. One of these took place in February 1915 in the shape of a drama symposium at which A. P. Wilson, the Scots manager of the Abbey Theatre, later to produce for the Players, expressed his opinion that a Scottish drama movement would develop in the direction of "realistic plays of a peasant or folk character", and thus the national soul would be expressed. Wilson continued to favour the development of rustic plays and after he left his post as producer for the Players at the end of 1923, he expressed disappointment that no Doric drama had yet developed.

The Scottish National Players gave their first performance on 13 January 1921 in the Royal Institute, Glagow, when three plays — *Chatelard* by C. Stewart Black, *Cute McCheyne* by J. L. Waugh and A. P. Wilson, and *Glenforsa* by J. Brandane and A. W. Yuill — were performed and favourably received by the Press. Several other performances were given that year and in February 1922 the Scottish National Theatre Society was formed with the following objects:

(a) To take over the assets and liabilities of the Scottish National Players Committee of the Saint Andrew Society (Glasgow).

(b) To develop Scottish national drama through the productions by the Scottish National Players of plays of Scottish life and character.

(c) To encourage in Scotland a public taste for good drama of any type.

(d) To found a Scottish National Theatre.

It is worth noting that the emphasis here is on Scottish plays — objective (c) is not the main one, as it was with the Glasgow Rep. The Players did perform a few non-Scottish plays

— but not so few as to prevent criticism that by doing so they were betraying their ideals!

Having started on a provisional basis, it had been felt necessary to establish the venture on a firm working one with permanent offices and rehearsal accommodation. The link with the St. Andrew Society had therefore been amicably severed in September 1921 and the Players thenceforth pursued their own course.

In 1922 they performed for short periods in Glasgow, in January, March and November at the Athenaeum, and in May at the Pavilion. In addition, they played at Oban and Balmoral and in December appeared in London in *A Valuable Rival* by Neil F. Grant. On this occasion a dinner attended by theatrical celebrities and others was given for the Players. George Bernard Shaw, though unable to attend, sent an encouraging telegram:—

> *As I shall not be in London on the 29th, I cannot avail myself of your kind invitation to dine with the Scottish National Players. The unanimous refusal of the English people to establish an English national theatre must not discourage them. The Englishman is so modest on his own that he never believes anything English deserves to succeed or can succeed, but he is boundlessly credulous as to foreign possibilities.*

Throughout their existence, the Players gave short seasons in Glasgow spread out over the year and toured at other times. This was deliberate policy, as the Players sought to be a national rather than a regional group, but it was a policy which attracted some criticism from those who felt that their efforts should be concentrated in Glasgow, rather than spent touring throughout the Highlands. In addition to the regular performances given at the Athenaeum, and afterwards the Lyric, the Players gave performances at other Glasgow theatres. In May 1922 they presented *Luiffy* by J. L. Waugh and A. P. Wilson at the Pavilion, and in July 1924 *The Crystal Set* by J. H. Bone at the same theatre where they perhaps found a more popular audience than they were accustomed to (it is arguable that the plays presented at the Pavilion were more in the nature of variety sketches, and thus were readily acceptable). In 1925, and again in 1926, the Players performed Robert Bain's *James the First of Scotland* at the Theatre Royal, and in 1923 and 1926 *The Glen is Mine* by John Brandane at the King's. *The Glen is Mine*, easily the most successful of their plays, was toured throughout Scotland by a professional company in 1927.

The Players visited London three times — in 1922, 1923 and 1930. On the first occasion, as already stated, they presented *A Valuable Rival* by Neil F. Grant, and on the second a triple bill of J. F. Ferguson's *Campbell of Kilmohr*, *A Valuable Rival* and *Luiffy*, and on the third occasion they played *The Glen is Mine* for a fortnight. They also toured the Stoll music-hall circuit. Several visits were paid to Edinburgh; in 1923, for example, *The Glen is Mine* and Gordon Bottomley's *Gruach* were presented at the Lyceum. In addition, radio broadcasts were made on a number of occasions. The Players made a substantial contribution to broadcast drama in the early days of the BBC in Scotland.

By far the most important side of the Players' activities, apart from their seasons in Glasgow, were the country tours and one-night stands to which the company itself attached great significance. An article in the *Glasgow Herald* in January 1926 reported:

> *It has been said that the work of a national theatre cannot properly be restricted to one centre of activity; it must carry its work to the small town and village as well, and this it should do consistently and thoroughly. Recognising this, as well as the educational and social value of good drama worthily presented, the Carnegie United Kingdom Trust has generously guaranteed this tour against financial loss. This guarantee is part of a considered scheme by the Trust for bringing good drama within the reach of the smaller communities which cannot hope to support it on a purely commercial basis.*

Local communities were exhorted to give all their support to the company, which it was claimed was "the country's move-ment to establish a National Drama". Among the many places visited were Oban in 1922, Bridge of Allan, Perth and Dunoon in 1924, several towns and villages during a three-week tour in summer 1927 of Perthshire, Aberdeenshire and Fife (during which the company slept under canvas) and the Border towns in the course of another tour in 1929.

The actors who worked with the Players were amateurs or

semi-professional (although a good many later turned professional, and had successful careers), despite the efforts of some members of the committee to change this situation. These men, among them the dramatists James Bridie and John Brandane, believed that if the company were ever to be properly established it would have to become fully professional. The idea was to take the Athenaeum by the season, but the management committee did not care for this proposal nor did most of the actors, who were understandably nervous about giving up their jobs. A policy of two-night runs was adopted instead, and in that year, 1932, the Players gave only four programmes. Operations were formally suspended two years later.

Unlike the actors, the principal producers were engaged throughout on a professional basis. Among them were A. P. Wilson, Frank D. Clewlow, Elliot Mason, W. G. Fay, and the young Tyrone Guthrie. Wilson, who was a Scot, came to the Players from the Abbey Theatre and when he left them he went into film production. As well as producing Gordon Bottomley's *Gruach* — probably his most notable presentation — he wrote some short pieces for the company. Clewlow came from Birmingham Rep. and went to broadcasting in Australia. It was he who was responsible for directing the premiere of Robert Bain's *James the First of Scotland*. Elliot Mason was later to become an actress of some distinction in comedy while W. Fay was another recruit from the Abbey. The most distinguished producer the Players had was, of course, Guthrie. He stayed for two years, led the first summer camping tour in 1927, directed Bridie's first stage play to be performed, *The Sunlight Sonata* in 1928, and was later to write that some of his happiest professional memories were of his time in Glasgow.

Guthrie's connection with Scotland was renewed periodically. In particular he directed *The Three Estates* in the Assembly Hall during the 1948 (and subsequent) Edinburgh Festivals, the first occasion on which that venue was used for drama. It was an inspired choice for the presentation of Lindsay's masterpiece, and fitting that Guthrie should have employed a number of actors who had begun with the Scottish National Players. Guthrie also had a continuing relationship with James Bridie, and was responsible for the first presentation of a Bridie play in London, *The Anatomist* in 1930. Curiously enough, Guthrie's last visit to Scotland in 1968 was to direct a production of that play at the Glasgow Citizens' Theatre by way of tribute to the actor Duncan Macrae.

Turning now to the drama performed by the Players, it is proposed to look at two of the most important writers whose work was regularly presented and then in the next chapter at lesser writers, paying particular attention to those whose plays were among the most popular. The dramatists chosen for consideration first of all are John Brandane and George Reston Malloch — Brandane because his work typifies exceptionally well the light, undemanding but effective type of play which predominated in the Players' repertoire, and Malloch because part of his work represents the kind of play which, although it did not figure very largely in the repertoire, exemplifies an important strand in Scottish dramatic writing whose potential has yet to be fully exploited.

John Brandane (Dr. John McIntyre) was born in 1869 in Bute. While working as a clerk in Glasgow he studied part-time and qualified as a doctor in 1901. Thereafter he practised in various parts of the United Kingdom and finally settled in Glasgow. He died in 1947. Brandane made a two-fold contribution to the work of the Players. In the first place he took a leading part in running the company's affairs and he also wrote a number of plays which were performed by them. These included several one-acters — *Glenforsa, The Spanish Galleon* (both written with A. W. Yuill), *Rory Aforesaid,* — and several full-length pieces — *The Glen is Mine , The Treasure Ship, The Lifting, The Inn of Adventure* and *Heather Gentry.* Only *Rory Aforesaid* was not premiered by the Players.

The most immediately striking feature of Brandane's work is that he invariably chooses Highland settings. The magical attraction of the Highlands is of course apparent in many other modern Scottish writers — for example Neil Munro and more recently Neil Gunn, in whose novels an altogether harsher world is depicted. The one exception to this generalisation as far as Brandane's plays are concerned is *The Happy War,* a one-acter set in the Haute Marne at the end of the First World War. Two of his plays — *The Treasure Ship* and *Rory Aforesaid* — are set in the fictitious West Highland town of Torlochan; one — *Heather Gentry* — in Drimfearn, another fictitious geographical location; and four — *The Glen is Mine, The Lifting, The Inn of Adventure* and *Glenforsa* — in Eilean Aros, which Brandane tells us is somewhere in the Inner Hebrides. This is obviously the island of Mull where Brandane spent several happy years as a doctor. *The Spanish Galleon*, which deals with the historical incident of the sinking of one of the ships of the Spanish Armada off Tobermory, is naturally set in Tobermory. Brandane's novels — *The Captain More* and *My Lady of Aros* (*The Inn of Adventure* is a theatrical adaptation of the former) — are also set in Eilean Aros.

It is interesting that Brandane, who wrote almost exclusively for an urban audience, should choose to set his plays in a part of Scotland still regarded as something of an unspoilt paradise. Brandane (a native of Bute and hence not strictly a Highlander) caters in his work, perhaps unconsciously, for the longing to escape to Arcadia which afflicts urban man. He was doing in the theatre what a number of glossy publications still do today for a Lowland urban readership. It is not difficult to deduce Brandane's attitude to the inhabitants of the Highlands from his plays. The Highlander is apparently a man given to sudden bursts of passion: in *Glenforsa* the two young lairds, Glenforsa and Oskamull, take to dicing and in a short time draw swords on each other. Elspeth, the heroine, having prevented any harm being done, acts as a mouthpiece for Brandane when she says "Weary fa' this hot Highland blood". Philip Linnell, hero of *The Inn of Adventure*, who is out to clear the name of his father as a cheat, constantly loses his temper, particularly when talking to Ardow, the son of the man who had accused his father of cheating. This, of course, is not surprising in the circumstances, but it occurs so frequently and intensely that one becomes conscious of the playwright's conviction that Highlanders are particularly given to such outbursts.

There also runs throughout Brandane's plays the suggestion that the Highlander is different from the Lowlander in his propensity for rather bizarre behaviour. Mrs Fraser, a Lowlander, at one point in *The Treasure Ship*, says of her husband: "Oh let him be! He's aye up to some nonsense. He's Highland ye ken".

The sentiment is often repeated in this particular play and finds an echo in, for example, *The Glen is Mine* when Colonel Murray says to Gallety, a Lowlander: "I've just been telling your wife that you'll soon get used to our ways in the Highlands — the drams and all that — a bit queer at first, eh?"

We may deduce that Brandane's view of the Highlands and its inhabitants is rather a superficial one. Most of the characters who people his plays are rather flat and hackneyed caricatures, drawn from melodrama and farce rather than from any study of the life. As such they are predictable and not very interesting. *The Glen is Mine*, however, is an exception to this stricture. Angus MacKinnon, the central character, although falling into the loveable Highland rascal stereotype, has greater intelligence that his author's other creations and can turn his mind to more than avoiding paying bills or screwing money out of people (although he does a fair amount of this too). And MacPhedran, the rapacious, sycophantic village trader, with his obsequious "Take care of yourself — Good people are scarce", has more individuality than most of Brandane's other characters. The dramatis personae of *The Glen is Mine* gain substantially from the fact that the play is about something; it has a recognisable theme which is more than can honestly be said for most of its author's other works.

The Glen is Mine (25 January 1923, Athenaeum) is undoubtedly Brandane's best play. Its theme is quite simply the future of the Highlands. Should they remain an unspoilt (and perhaps depopulated) paradise or should they be industrialised? Colonel Murray, the proprietor of Ardsheilach and Coillemore, has handed over his estate to his son Charlie in order to avoid death duties ("There's government for ye! There's poaliticks! The big thiefs!" Brandane has one character comment naively). Charlie, unknown to his father, has hired an iron prospector who has found a seam which could be profitably worked. Charlie proposes therefore to start an iron-mine and makes this clear to his father when the latter discovers his plans.

Charlie puts forward the point of view that the Highlands should be exploited for whatever mineral wealth they possess, whereas his father believes this would be a desecration — or so it seems. Unfortunately Brandane detracts from the integrity of Charlie's point of view by having him admit to needing the money. We are left at the end wondering whether Charlie really believes in the development of the Highlands, or is merely interested in recouping his financial losses. However, at times in the play Charlie does seem to be advocating the mine for non-personal reasons. He points out that it would put an end to the shabby manoeuvres of lairds to make ends meet, but

Brandane again detracts from the impact of his remarks by having him abuse the crofters, an action which would probably alienate an audience otherwise sympathetic to Charlie's point of view. It emerges further that Charlie proposes to use water power in his scheme and this involves the eviction of an old crofter, Angus MacKinnon, from his land. The scales of sympathy are by now a little bit weighted against Charlie. The Colonel is concerned to emphasise the social price of industrialisation and this is something which is taken up by Angus and his prospective son-in-law, Murdo, in their discussions of the subject. Angus feels the ironworks will ruin the countryside, whereas Murdo sees them as bringing "life", "knowledge", "science" and opportunity:

I ken I'm fit for something better than an odd-man's job
at Torlochan Hotel. Driving — fencing — sheep-shearing
— peat lifting.
Tach! The life of a slave!

Murdo's problem is (still) the young Highlander's problem — how can he find a job in the Highlands for which his abilities fit him? When Morag, Angus's daughter, objects that the iron mine would destroy the old Highland ways, Murdo replies —

The good old Highland ways! Three o'clock of a cold morning and up the hill to the lambing. Bringing the mails over Kellan cliffs when the snow's drifted yards deep. Driving the Doctor to Moy, thirty mile and back, when the North wind's skelping down the sound. That's the good old ways for Murdo Mackay!

What Brandane is saying through Murdo is that the good old Highland ways can mean a miserable existence. Angus, however, sticks to his point and tells Jock Gallety, the farmer who has come from Ayrshire, that the pattern of living in Glasgow is not at all desirable and that it would have been better for the people of Eilean Aros to stick completely to the old Highland ways. "Aweel", says Jock, "there's twa sides to every story", and this seems to be Brandane's ultimate attitude. He fails to resolve the dramatic conflict he has set up, and jouks out of it by means of a series of contrived *dei ex machina*: Charlie abandons his plans for the mine since Redfern the prospector has decided to proceed no further; he also finds that the other lairds are down on him when they hear how he is trying to bankrupt Angus to have him evicted, and he realizes that his fiancee might not think very much of such dealings if she were to hear of them; finally Murdo comes into a croft and forgets about "civilization" and "knowledge". So at the end of the play Angus can go off "into the sunlight and the breeze" rather banally playing on his pipes *The Glen is Mine*.

A critic at the time said of the language of *The Glen is Mine* that it has an "exquisite Celtic idiom, as pure and expansive as Synge's use of the Anglo-Irish speech". This is fanciful. The language of *The Glen is Mine* is business-like English with little or nothing which is not plain and matter-of-fact, although there is an attempt to suggest the Highland idiom where that is appropriate.

Brandane indeed often strives after poetic effects by the use of Gaelic phrases; many of the people he is writing about, in both his historical and his contemporary plays, may well have spoken Gaelic, but the Scottish Players audience did not. So, one could argue, Brandane incorporates Gaelic phrases in the interests of being true to life. It is doubtful if this is the case. Brandane, one suspects, uses Gaelic in an attempt to heighten his language and to add to the 'romantic charm' of the plays. Phrases like *Mo Chridhe, Ochanee*, or *Mo thruaigh* may sound impressive to a non-Gaelic audience but it is the impression of ignorance. Brandane is using these phrases to bolster up his rather undistinguished dialogue — the number of times a character declares 'my pain and my longing' or something of the sort in Brandane's more serious pieces is depressingly frequent.

Brandane's inability to write well in his dramatic pieces is counter-balanced by the language of his comedies, which is unpretentious and functional. *The Glen is Mine* has some dialogue which is lively and conversational, as have its author's other comedies. Only on rare occasions does he write in a stilted fashion in the comedies.

The final verdict on John Brandane's work must be that it does not represent a very great contribution to the Scottish theatre. At best his plays, in particular *The Glen is Mine*, do attempt to come to grips with the life of Scotland, although they do not go very far in this direction, principally because they are plays which do not often confront historical or contemporary reality. On the other hand, Brandane has a considerable gift for creating lively, if at times frenetic, theatrical action and sustaining it for two and a half hours.

George Reston Malloch was born in Elderslie, Renfrewshire, in 1875 and was educated at Paisley Grammar School and privately. Malloch's literary efforts were not confined to the drama. He published several volumes of poetry, contributed short stories to various magazines and acted as dramatic critic for newspapers in Holland and this country. It was in this latter capacity that he appeared in the pages of *The Scottish Nation*, one of the period's short-lived publications edited by C. M. Grieve (Hugh MacDiarmid), which was published for some seven months during 1923. There is a distinct social bias in Malloch's criticism and sarcastic comments on "well-fed audiences" appear not infrequently in it. He died in London in 1953.

The Scottish National Players performed five of Malloch's plays, three one-acters — *Thomas the Rhymer, The House of the Queen* and *The Grenadier* — and two full-length plays — *Soutarness Water* and *The Coasts of India*. Only *The Grenadier* was not a premiere. He wrote several other plays which can be traced — *Arabella, Prologue to Flodden, The Still Folk* — the last two being one-act plays — and *Down in the Forest*.

Apart from *The Grenadier*, a bleak little one-acter, *Soutarness Water* (19 January 1926, Athenaeum) is the first play of Malloch's to merit serious consideration. It was performed by the Players apparently after a great deal of heart-searching on the part of the committee, which was rather worried about the impact of a play which has as its climax an incestuous marriage. The committee knew its audience well, for it appears that the spectators reacted disapprovingly to blasphemy in the second act, a reaction which was really against the entire spirit of the play.

Malloch prefaces *Soutarness Water* by quoting on 'Old Scots Rhyme':

> *Tweed said to Till,*
> *"What gars ye rin sae still?"*
> *Till said to Tweed,*
> *"Though ye rin wi' speed,*
> *And I rin slow,*
> *When ye drown ae man,*
> *I drown twa"*

The grim fatalistic atmosphere engendered by these lines pervades the entire play. In the first act Hugh Munro has an argument with his widowed mother over his courting of and proposed marriage to Jean Dochart, daughter of Andrew Dochart of the Mains, who, Mrs Munro says, is a loose woman. The parish minister, Mr MacPhail, arrives while they are arguing and, when Hugh leaves for the Mains, MacPhail warns him not to return late if he is proposing to use the stepping stones across Soutarness Water which runs outside the Munros' house. When Hugh has gone, Mrs Munro tells MacPhail that Jean Dochart's mother, who is now dead, had been her husband's mistress and, when the two parted to marry different people, Jean McIntyre, as she was then, 'ill-wisht' old Hugh for breaking up the relationship. "Ill or well, trickle or spate, Soutarness Water 'ull get ye yet", she apparently said to him, and these lines, repeated throughout the play, give specific relevance to the 'Old Scots Rhyme'. Munro was drowned in Soutarness Water but the minister insists that this is merely coincidence and says he is shocked that Mrs Munro believes in such nonsense. After the minister's departure, Daft Jock, the local half-wit, enters and in the course of conversation tells Mrs Munro that Mrs Dochart of the Mains was his mother. As the noise of the stream increases he hysterically demands to be let out of the house. Left to herself, Mrs Munro, worried that Hugh went without her blessing, decides to go across Soutarness Water to meet him. After she exits, there is a cry. She has, of course, been drowned.

A large part of Act II, which takes place on the day of Mrs Munro's funeral, is occupied by Andrew Dochart's reflections, prompted by whisky, on his past life and on religion. He tells Daft Jock that he was once a staunch church-man but he has left the Kirk since he has lost his faith in God. Later he tells Innes and Robson, formerly two of his fellow-elders, how Jean McIntyre had, unknown to Dochart, been compelled to marry him when he settled a debt of her father's — after Hugh Munro jilted her to marry a woman with more money than Jean. Jean kept seeing Munro and young Jean is their daughter. So young Hugh is about to marry his step-sister. The elders do not give Dochart much help in his terrible dilemma, and he seems about to tell Jean and Hugh something of the truth when he is suddenly paralysed by a stroke.

The third act takes place on the wedding day of Jean and

Hugh. Andrew Dochart, still paralysed and speechless from his stroke, watches the proceedings from a wheel-chair. When the minister comes to the 'impediment' clause Daft Jock interrupts: "wha wadna lauch tae see a man merrit tae his ain sister?" The wedding is abandoned, and events move to their grim conclusion — Jean drowns herself in Soutarness Water and Hugh shoots himself.

Much of Malloch's earlier dramatic writing is stodgy and untheatrical; it is only just therefore to say that this is not the case with *Soutarness Water*, for its dialogue moves smoothly and dramatically:

HUGH: A'm for oot.

MRS MUNRO: An' whaur may ye be gaun'?

HUGH: Oh, A'll just tak' a donner roon'

MRS MUNRO: Ye needna think tae deceive me.

HUGH: A'm no wantin' tae deceive ye, mither, but ye kin o' ask for it.

MRS MUNRO: Hugh Munro, that's nae wey tae speak to your mither. A ken fine whit's in your mind.

HUGH: Weel, an' if you do, whit wey dae ye speir at me? There's nae deceit aboot me, naturally, but if A wis tae say A wis gaun' ower tae the Mains there'd be a fine to-do.

MRS MUNRO: An' maybe there'd be call for it. A'm no' wantin' ony lass frae the Mains brocht intae your father's hoose as his son's wife. Ye ken ma mind aboot it onyway.

Soutarness Water could well be described as a Calvinist play, not merely because a large part of the play is devoted to a discussion of the doctrine of predestination — the idea that some souls have been marked down for salvation and some for perdition before they take human form — but also because the events of the play do imply a pattern of fate into which the characters must inevitably fit, whether they like it or not. Admittedly, the starting point of the play's grim events is the curse Jean McIntyre places on Hugh Munro, and one could argue that it is the dark forces thus invoked which are responsible for the catastrophe, and not predestination. But there is an obvious correlation between the idea of predestination and the notion that after a curse certain events are ordained, although it is not a correlation that Malloch explores to the full. Calvinism and a belief in the power of curses are not incompatible bedfellows — far from it.

The minister in the play is at least of an enlightened disposition and does not seem to believe in either evil powers or in predestination. The irony of the events for him is that they appear to prove that there are malevolent powers at work intent on destroying human happiness. Neither he nor the kindly elder Robson, a man who openly voices his doubts about predesination, is able to prevent the catastrophe. Innes, another elder, hard unsympathetic character as he is, seems much nearer the truth when he alludes to the "sins o' the faithers" being visited on the children — although Innes had earlier suggested to Dochart that he stop the wedding. That Dochart is prevented from doing so by his stroke seems to bear out Innes's own professed belief in predestination, in the face of which human beings are powerless.

In one speech Dochart seems to be condemning the abuse of religion to sanctify something intrinsically evil — for example, the death of the soldiers of an enemy nation — but Malloch has him pursue his thoughts further when he places a whisky bottle in front of the two elders, Innes and Robson:

> For jist conseeder the power o' that bottle! It mak's bad
> men feel guid an' fu' o' soft repentance. It mak's guid men
> bad and fu' o' anger an' a' sorts o' unrighteousness. It can
> mak' the wise intae fools an' fools as happy as the wise. It
> mak's guid lassies intae whores an' gars whores think
> themselves guid lassies. There's black murders in that
> gowden bottle, an' prisons an' the gallows; a' the dark
> thrills o' lust, an' hatred, an' weans buried under a hedge
> i' the mirk o' nicht. Aye, there's madness in it an' ripe
> wisdom, an' folly an' tears. It has power over a' men and
> weemen. See — A pit it there in the centre o' the board tae
> preside owre the Session, like the Holy Spirit ye and the
> Minister is sae fond o' askin' tae descend on yer
> deleeberations. Whit does it stand for saintly sirs? Whit
> could it stand for but God Himsel', since its power is
> unbounded an' brings as much meesery intae the warld as
> His does.

By his identification of the power of God with the evil power of whisky, Malloch (for the events of the play bear out what

Dochart is saying) is not only suggesting that the Calvinist God is in truth an evil one, but also seems to be going on to suggest, as Bridie was later to do in *The Queen's Comedy*, that God, or the power which orders human destinies in the world, is essentially malevolent.

There are faults in *Soutarness Water*. Not all of the dialect is convincing, some of the events of the play are a little too melodramatic, and Malloch's ideas could have been presented in a clearer fashion, but it remains a play which must rank high in the achievement of the Scottish drama this century — it is a truly Scottish play, not because it is set in Scotland, but because its principal and subordinate concerns are rooted in the Scottish psyche.

The Coasts of India (23 October 1928, Lyric) is also a play worthy of attention. It concerns itself with the aspirations of its principal characters towards more satisfying lives than they are able to have. The heroine of the play is Marion Mair, the daughter of a mill owner. Talking to Gray, an employee of her father's who has been dismissed because he stated the case for a wage increase a little too strongly for Mair's liking, Marion learns of all his frustrated hopes, and of how he would have liked to have joined his brother who is an engineer on a boat which sails on "the coasts of India". Marion is struck by this phrase which seems to her to embody all her own aspirations. The theme of the play is that life rarely allows us to reach the coasts of India. Marion, very much the Shavian woman, is unable to study as a doctor since her father's business is forced to close down, and at the end of the play, rather than wearily go on working and studying part time to become a teacher, she accepts a proposal of marriage from an old but persistent suitor. Her acceptance of this is seen as a defeat for her desire to be independent. Several of the other characters find their hopes of life curtailed in a similar manner, among them Marion's cousin Tom who ends up as a coal salesman.

Other concerns are touched on in the play but not developed: Malloch introduces the theme of industrial conflict but then drops it; the relationship between the sexes could bear deeper examination than he gives it; his presentation of old Mair in financial difficulties, after his business collapses, is some-what comic (Mair is, for example, shocked to learn that his wife now shops at the Co-op) although the effects of such a change of fortune are reasonably well conveyed.

The major limitation of the play is its undistinguished language — a stilted English rather than the vigorous Scots dialect of *Soutarness Water* — which continually detracts from the impact that it might otherwise have. Its great merit, however, is that Malloch as in *Soutarness Water* deals with recognisable human experience and does not invite us to escape to some non-existent Scottish fairy land. That in the end is Malloch's durable achievement.

CHAPTER SIX
The Minor Dramatists

IT IS OF COURSE DIFFICULT to survey accurately and fairly the wide range of drama performed by the Players — one hundred and thirty-one plays were presented, half for the first time. However, some idea of their quality can be gained by considering the most frequently performed one-act and full-length plays. A list of the ten most popular plays in each category is given below (eleven in the case of one-acters since the final two had an equal number of performances):

ONE-ACT PLAYS	Author	Performances
A Valuable Rival	Neil F. Grant	208
*C'Est La Guerre**	Morland Graham	80
*The Scarecrow**	J. A. Ferguson	63
*Luiffy**	J. L. Waugh & A. P. Wilson	58
*The Dawn**	Naomi Jacob	46
*Cute McCheyne**	J. L. Waugh & A. P. Wilson	45
*The Crystal Set**	J. H. Bone	42
*The Poacher**	Joe Corrie	40
*The Mother**	George Blake	35
Campbell of Kilmohr	J. A. Ferguson	29
The Grenadier	G. Reston Malloch	29

FULL-LENGTH PLAYS	Author	Performances
*The Glen is Mine**	John Brandane	105
*Ayont the Hill**	Cormac Simpson	63
*S for Sugar Candy**	Donald McLaren	49
*The Flower in the Vase**	Cormac Simpson	37
*The Beannachy Bomb**	Hal. D. Stewart	32
*A Month of Sundays**	Hal D. Stewart	31
*Walls of Jericho**	Robert Kemp	30
*Clyde-Built**	George Blake	28
*Brief Harmony**	Moultrie R, Kelsall	28
Late Christopher Bean	Emlyn Williams	28

(*signifies premiere*)

It is our intention to make some observations on most of these plays (*Walls of Jericho* will be discussed when Robert Kemp's work is considered in a later chapter, and the *Late Christopher Bean* will not be discussed, for it was performed late in the Players career and is not typical of their output). Interestingly enough, Bridie's plays, which will also be considered later, were not among the most successful performed by the Players in that for all that eight of his plays were presented by them, the average number of performances per play was only six, a very low figure compared to those attained by other pieces in the Players' repertoire. Bridie tended to give apprentice work to the Glasgow company — they premiered four of his early plays — and as he established himself in London and elsewhere the Players had to content themselves with presenting his plays after they had been premiered. Given Bridie's feelings about the importance of the Players turning professional, it is not surprising that this situation developed.

Turning now to the most frequently performed work we see that the most popular play presented was the one-act *A Valuable Rival* by Neil F. Grant; but before dealing with it a word or two ought to be said about the one-act form itself. The one-act play was extremely popular during the nineteenth century and served as a kind of appetiser before the main dramatic fare of the evening. More often than not it took the form of a farcical comedy, but on occasion it was more demanding. Its importance in the professional theatre declined at the beginning of the twentieth century as the unaccompanied full-length play became the norm. It is worthy of note, however, that some of the most interesting work at the Glasgow Repertory Theatre, and indeed the two plays praised most highly in an earlier chapter, took the form of one-acters: *Jean*, which accompanied Pinero's *Dandy Dick* at the Royalty, and *Campbell of Kilmohr*, which was one item in a triple bill which also included two of Shaw's one-act plays.

The one-act form has seen a revival in recent years, particularly in the small club theatres where double bills and triple bills are more acceptable than they would be in a larger theatre. Of course such one-acters are often vehicles more for experiment than anything else, and that is why they are suitable for the club theatre which tends to attract a more dedicated audience than the repertory or commercial theatre. It is interesting to see how a theatrical form has changed from being the medium for harmless diversion to being a vehicle for avant-garde experimentation. It ought also to be added that the one-act form may not be in a particularly flourishing state in the British theatre but in radio and television it is the most common form which plays take, with the half-hour, forty-five-minute, and one-hour play much more in evidence that the two- or three-hour one, even in that haven of cultural experiment, Radio 3.

In the inter-war period the one-act play became very much the amateur genre. Indeed it can be argued that the amateur movement gave a new lease of life to a form that was facing extinction. The attractions of the one-act play to amateurs are obvious: it is much less demanding of acting and production talent than a full-length play; it is ideally suited to the kind of situation where amateur groups are called upon to make some kind of contribution to a concert or similar entertainment. The introduction of the one-act play festivals reinforced the amateur predilection for the form. The first festival was organised in Scotland by the Scottish Community Drama Association in 1926 and it has continued ever since, although in recent years homespun plays have given way to some extent in favour of more cosmopolitan work. The trouble with the one-act play of course is that, except in the most accomplished hands, it is really only a starting point for more sustained writing, and unfortunately the amateur movement's appetite for one-act plays may well have prevented the growth of particular writers who found that they could attain a substantial if limited following and annual acclaim by sticking to the form.

A Valuable Rival (11 May 1914, Criterion Theatre, London) is in many ways typical of the genre. Jameson, the old proprietor of a newspaper in Sweno, a small Northern Scottish town, is apparently worried about the competition from another recently-formed paper, run by a man called Bain. His daughter, Maggie, has discovered a forged letter which Bain had used some years previously to further his career. Bain is summoned and it looks as if Jameson is going to destroy him, but the older man burns the incriminating letter because he values the competition which Bain provides — he has been most unhappy since he smashed his previous competitors. When Maggie protests, after Bain has left, he warns her that unless she desists, he will tell the world of her infatuation for Bain, an infatuation which he has discovered and which the audience probably guessed before this revelation.

It is not a play of any great account, but its success can probably be at least partially explained by the way in which theatrical interest is maintained and by the curiosity which the characterisation of Maggie might arouse in the audience, although the author's psychological insight is limited.

Morland Graham's *C'Est La Guerre* (21 October 1926, Lyric), another popular one-act, is a touching little play set in France during the 1914-1918 war. Jock Broon, a soldier from Shotts, helps Marie, a French girl who has been wounded, by bandaging her arm. They talk in a mixture of languages and we can sense the beginning of a relationship between them before Jock leaves Marie and her father while they are asleep. The play, the effect of which depends on the ordinariness of the people involved, is rather spoiled by making Marie an actress who has played Shakespeare's Juliet in Paris.

J. A. Ferguson's *The Scarecrow* (21 October 1921, Arts League of Service, Maidstone) is set in Inverness-shire in the early nineteenth century. Not this author's best work, it deals with a ruse employed by a man on the run from the police: he disguises himself as a scarecrow. By way of balance, mention should be made here of Ferguson's *The King of Morven* (21 October 1926, Lyric), a very unromantic play about the Highlands, premiered by the Players. The action takes place in the house of McAskill, a factor who is responsible for 'clearing' an estate. His wife is very unhappy about the situation. A tinker arrives, ostensibly to sell delf, and talks — much to McAskill's annoyance — about the empty cottages he has found on his way. Tension develops to such an extent in the house that McAskill walks out and tells three sailors that the tinker is a wanted criminal. Mrs McAskill tries to prevent the sailors from press-ganging the tinker, but as McAskill denies that she is his wife, both she and the tinker are carried off. This is a dramatic play that gives grim expression to the author's view of the Clearances. McAskill is a man so corrupted by the evil that he is doing that he is prepared to see his own wife abducted.

Luiffy (20 December 1921, Athenaeum) and *Cute McCheyne* (13 January 1921, Royal Institute, Glasgow) were adaptations by A. P. Wilson of short stories by J. L. Waugh. Both are character studies with little real dramatic interest and are rural in background.

The Dawn (13 November 1923, Athenaeum) by Naomi Jacob takes us into the romantic world of Highland myth. Two old people are reminiscing about the '45 in which their son has been killed. A mysterious traveller arrives and it is soon obvious as he talks of his trials with a gloomy sentimentality and looks forward to "the dawn" that he is the Young Pretender. It is a play of little life or dramatic force.

J. H. Bone's *The Crystal Set* (7 July 1924, Pavilion) also has a rural background, although a contemporary one. It is set in a village in Renfrewshire and concerns the efforts of Willie to listen to his crystal radio set despite the interruptions of Grace, his wife, and Granny. However, his efforts are of no avail for he inadvertently smashes the set himself. It is a very slight play which, despite the apparent modernity of the crystal set, has about it an archaic quality, which is of course reinforced by the use of dialect.

Only two of Joe Corrie's plays were performed by the Players. This is rather surprising for he was a most prolific writer, producing over fifty one-act plays, a much smaller number of full-length ones, a novel and several volumes of verse. He began writing while working as a miner in Fife, and not surprisingly this background shows in the plays. *The Shillin' A Week Man* (22 March 1927, Lyric), a one-acter, deals with the efforts of a Mrs Paterson to avoid the Shillin' A Week Man to whom she owes money. She hides in the back-room while her daughter tells the collector she is in Kirkcaldy. The collector becomes extremely angry, discovers Mrs Paterson and threatens to have her husband's wages stopped. At this point Paterson arrives, having just been paid off and, despite his wife's efforts, finds out about the debt. The play ends rather anti-climactically with Paterson telling his wife to pay sixpence a week when she can. There is in the play a sense of poverty, which is brought out in small things such as the borrowing of tea, and in larger things such as redundancy, strikes, and the shillin' a week system itself. This sense of poverty is also found in a more deliberately humorous play, *The Poacher* (21 October 1926, Lyric), whose title clearly indicates its subject matter. It comes across, for example, when the hero tries to coax money from his wife and also in a speech by him about the injustices of society. Unfortunately Corrie displays in the play a fatal tendency to aim for laughs at all costs, a tendency which continually stunted his growth as a dramatist.

It is unfortunately true that Corrie's later development took him away from his own professed aim, as expressed in the magazine *Scottish Stage* in April 1931: "the drama should deal with life, and the state of our environment has so much to do with life that we cannot ignore it on the stage. We must show the worst that is in us to bring out the best that is in us which means being ruthless and cruel and offensive". For all that he does on occasion reflect the hard and bitter struggles of ordinary working people in his plays, most of his output is of the Scots comedy variety, and indeed Corrie's name has come to be identified with a particular kind of Scots comedy which is set in rural Scotland and has couthy characters who speak the Doric. There is little recognition of the realities of modern life at all. The form is usually that of the one act play of which Corrie, to be fair, is a reasonably accomplished practitioner.

Corrie was of course writing for a market, that of the amateurs. His plays went down well, and still do, at one-act festivals, women's guilds and similar gatherings. In a sense Corrie was ruined by the amateur movement for it limited him formally and encouraged him in seeking the easy laugh and the neat solution. It is hard to disagree with Bridie's verdict on both Corrie and T. M. Watson, another dramatist who, after making brave statements about "plays which kick orthodoxy in the pants and sail as near to the blasphemy and obscenity laws as possible", proceeded to turn out amusing but empty Scots comedies, his most successful being *Bachelors are Bold* and *Beneath the Wee Red Lums*. Bridie said during a talk to the Royal Philosophical Society of Glasgow in 1949:

> *If I am asked whether I admire Messrs Corrie and Watson, I reply that I do; and that I continually mourn over them and pray that they may see the light. It is as if Dickens and Thackeray, knowing themselves to be masters of the anecdote, had written nothing but magazine stories till the greater constructive virtue went out of them. If I were in the mood for casting blame, I should blame the SCDA Festivals for robbing Scotland of two rare dramatists. They are not the only ones.* (Dramaturgy in Scotland)

George Blake, to whose work we now turn, was a man of

undoubted talent. Leaving school in Greenock, he embarked on a study of law which was interrupted by the First World War. After the war he went into journalism and joined the *Glasgow Evening News*. He then went to London and became in succession editor of *John o'London's*, editor of the *Strand Magazine* and a director of Faber and Faber, the publishers. In 1932 he returned to Scotland where he remained, pursuing the careers of journalism, broadcasting and writing. He was a prolific writer, producing novels — of which the best known is probably *The Shipbuilders* — and a variety of non-fiction books.

Blake is a man with a reputation for writing honestly about urban Scotland. He contributed *The Mother* and *Clyde-Built* to the Scottish Players. *The Mother* (13 April 1921, Royal Institute, Glasgow) however falls into the category of plays about the hot-blooded Highlander, of which Brandane was so fond. The play is set in a croft at a place called Ardlamey. Morag Gillespie, the tenant of the croft, is told in the first scene by Catto, the laird's factor, that she must give up her house since the laird wants it. Catto, it emerges, is really the father of Morag's son, Alastair. In the second scene the laird arrives and reiterates to Morag that she must leave her home. Alastair, who has discovered the truth about Catto, bursts in and murders him. He flees for his life and at the end of the play Old Callum, Morag's father-in-law, is left muttering — as he has done throughout — "There was aye a Gillespie in Ardlamey". The piece could not be described as tragic, though it has dramatic power; but it lacks the depth of characterization necessary to engage an audience's feelings at all substantially.

Clyde-Built (23 November 1922, Athenaeum), a full-length play, is centred on the Crockett family, the owners of an old-established Greenock firm of lifeboat builders which is facing bankruptcy. Ruin can only be avoided if the firm is bought up by Mersons, an English firm which has Jewish connections. The price that the Crocketts have to pay is the marriage of Old Crockett's grand-daughter, Jean, whose father has been lost at sea, to Stanley Merson, the son of the owner of Mersons. Jean's mother does not favour this match under-standably, nor does she want her daughter to marry her own choice, Harry Douglas, a sea captain, on account of his hazardous occupation. Jean's mother is contrasted with her Aunt Helen, a social climber, who is very much in favour of her niece marrying Merson. However, at the critical moment — when Harry Douglas is feared drowned and Jean has agreed to the marriage — Douglas returns denouncing the jerry-built Merson ship which sank beneath him and praising the lifeboats which saved his life, every one from the Crockett yard. Old Crockett, on hearing this, decides that he prefers ruin to an alliance with Merson, and tears up the merger agreement.

There is a strong moral conflict in the play, and Blake engages our sympathy for Old Crockett in his dilemma, although the characterization is somewhat lacking in depth. The play is also at times redolent with the Wha's Like Us attitude and there are distinctly xenophobic overtones. However, it must be said that *Clyde-Built* is nevertheless a well-constructed and dramatically interesting play.

Cormac Simpson, who began writing under the encouragement of Alfred Wareing, spent most of his life teaching in London and this seems to have encouraged in him a romantic nostalgia for Scotland which is apparent in his plays. The central character in *The Flower in the Vase* (25 December 1928, Lyric), Irene Erndom, decides to forsake London and the fashionable marriage her mother has arranged for a farmhouse near Aberfoyle. The contrast between the metropolis and the country is constantly emphasized to the latter's advantage in rather undistinguished language — at one point, for example, Irene refers to "the green world calling me home out of the smooth, hot, dusty desert". The anti-urban theme is apparent too in *Ayont the Hill* (22 March 1927, Lyric); John Kerr, an old farmer, suddenly decides that he wants a change of life, and despite the advice of family and friends forsakes his farm and his wife, who is unwilling to accompany him, for London. He is of course disillusioned with the metropolis and returns repentant to the farm. There is a little subsidiary interest in the play — Kerr's daughter has a romance with the local vet, his son Rob departs for Canada and Mr Comrie, the estate agent, declares his adulation for Mrs Kerr — but it does not add up to very much.

S. For Sugar Candy (17 November 1938, Lyric) by Donald McLaren is effective if routine comedy. David Coggie and his brother, Sir Peter, run a confectionery firm. Sir Peter is very conscious of having risen in the world and has acquired the appurtenances of gentility including a butler, much to his brother's annoyance. Into this situation comes Tabitha, daughter of the third, long-lost Coggie brother, who together with Budge, the butler, reorganises the household, saves the firm from Jewish cut-throats and becomes engaged to the butler's son who is thereafter installed as works manager. Although mildly amusing, *S. for Sugar Candy* commands little attention.

Hal D. Stewart, who was a frequent extoller of the virtues of the middlebrow in a succession of articles in the theatrical press, wrote several plays for the Players, one-act and full-length. *The Beannachy Bomb* (11 August 1937, Lundin Links), a full-length play, is set in the Macdonald Arms in Beannachy, a small Highland town. Colin Macdonald, the proprietor's son, is supposed to be looking after the hotel during his father's absence in hospital, and the play revolves around the attempts by the new maid, Isa Brodie, to improve the hotel. It turns out in the end that Isa has been sent by her mother — who owns a string of Glasgow tearooms — to spy out the land, and as a result her mother buys her way into the Macdonald Arms. There is much activity, including a mountain rescue and romance — Colin, having almost succumbed to the charms of a lady artist from Glasgow, marries Isa in the end. *The Beannachy Bomb* is a cocktail which Isa invents. Unfortunately, the play lacks characterization, plot and theatricality.

A Month of Sundays (19 August 1931, Earlsferry) is a better play. It is set in the small town of Netherbrae near Langholm. A new minister, Alan Forsyth, arrives and shatters the old-fashioned ideas of the community. He also becomes involved with a girl, Molly Carlyle, whose previous young man is so incensed that he seizes the opportunity to make trouble for Forsyth by bringing to Netherbrae the show-girl wife whom Forsyth thought was dead. After a struggle Forsyth wins his congregation back, but then to spite them he announces his intentions of going on the stage with his wife. The play is thin but, despite a wildly improbable ending, has some theatrical power. At the beginning of the action, it looks for the moment as if Stewart is going to develop as his theme the clash between traditional Presbyterianism and more modern ideas, but this unfortunately never happens.

Brief Harmony (16 August 1934, Earlsferry) by Moultrie Kelsall was an unpretentious light-hearted piece written for one of the Players' summer tours.

Of the dramatists who were not among the most popular a few deserve mention here. Gordon Bottomley, although not a Scot, took an active part in the development of the Scottish drama movement and had two verse plays performed by the Players. *Gruach* (20 March 1923, Athenaeum), premiered by them, tells how the Scottish king and Shakespearean hero Macbeth first met his wife. The play is set in Fortingall Castle. Conan, the thane, is to marry his cousin Gruach the following day, but Gruach it appears is a lone, brooding kind of woman, given to riding across moors at twilight and very unhappy at the prospect of marriage to Conan. Macbeth arrives en route to the Earl of Caithness, and Gruach and he are so attracted to each other that they ride off in the middle of the night, leaving Conan, who is unaware of what has happened, to mutter about his unease at the prospect of being married to Gruach. It is a play of a certain intensity and the verse, though at times stilted, is more than competent. Nonetheless the lack of any original insight by the author into his subject matter and the archaic use of verse combine to give the piece a second-hand quality.

Britain's Daughter (20 November 1922, Old Vic), is set during the Roman invasion of Britain. After an unsuccessful revolt against the Romans, Nest, heir to the throne of a British tribe, has been captured, whipped and tied to a post to await execution. Some of the other women accept the advances of Roman soldiers while others look forward to Nest's death. She herself declines a Roman general's offer to look after her, but is forcibly carried off to Gaul with other women prisoners at the end of the play, leaving behind a lamenting people, some of whom pity and some of whom curse her. There is a grim atmosphere created skilfully in the piece, although the verse is less effective than that of *Gruach*. However, it must be said that Bottomley is much more adept in the use of verse than any other of the Scottish Players' dramatists.

Robert Bain's verse play *James the First of Scotland* (11 May 1925, Theatre Royal), premiered by the Players, represents another genre of Scottish drama, one in which Robert Kemp has worked with some success, namely the play which centres on some great historical figure, in this case James I. James is represented as a just man trying to establish order in a country beset by querulous nobles; the play could well pass muster as a pageant, but it does not have the depth to make any higher claims. The blank verse Bain employs some of the time is unsuccessful, but his prose is often theatrically effective. Bain has obviously been influenced by Shakespeare's models not only in his use of blank verse but in the general structure of his play, the use of omens in the sky and the regular introduction of the 'common weal' into the action, a device that may also have been borrowed from *The Three Estates*.

Finally, a play much praised at the time was Murray McClymont's *The Mannoch Family*, initially premiered south of the border (26 February 1927, Birmingham Rep.) with Laurence Olivier in the lead. Peter Mannoch, a member of a well-to-do Borders family, is in love with Ailsa Stroan, the daughter of a local chicken farmer who warns Peter to keep away from his daughter. Mrs Mannoch — an excessively religiose, Old Testament-orientated widow — is totally opposed to the marriage, and it is only with an ill grace that she lets Ailsa into the home, when the girl arrives terrified after being beaten by her father. Likewise, she finds herself in conflict with her daughter Bee, who is about to run away with a married man. The climax comes when Stroan arrives to reclaim Ailsa and reveals that his elder daughter Grizel, who is now dead, was fathered by Clinton Mannoch, Mrs Mannoch's husband. Mrs Mannoch is shocked, though unrepentant in her opposition to her son's marriage which proceeds nonetheless. Bee having run off with the married man, she is left alone at the end of the play to read her Old Testament. *The Mannoch Family* is not an outstanding play, but its author does attempt to deal with the hypocrisies of Scottish Calvinism in an honest fashion and avoids the sentimentality of much Scottish rural drama. The characters are not altogether convincing, but do seem to be modelled rather less on stereotypes. One point worth noting is that the climax of the play is very similar to that of *Soutarness Water:* both plays deal with the contrast between apparent religious devotion and the drives, in both cases sexual, which lurk beneath it.

Having now considered a fair number of the plays which the Scottish National Players performed, we can perhaps draw certain conclusions. First of all, as one can only expect of a situation where dramatists are learning their job, many of the plays we have discussed lack theatricality. Not all the writers, however, fail in this respect. John Brandane was always conscious of the need to keep an audience interested in what is happening on stage. And in a writer like Malloch can be seen the growth of theatrical craftmanship: the early plays are static, whereas *Soutarness Water*, despite its long discussion passages, has real dramatic momentum.

On the whole the one-act plays are better constructed. *A Valuable Rival*, the most popular play produced, is designed to hold the audience's attention throughout and is never dull. The same can be said of other plays which have subject matter of little significance — their authors have taken the trouble to learn a little about stagecraft. It is as if the Scottish dramatists were learning through the simplest and most manageable form. The strain of attempting to sustain interest over two and a half hours is clear in many full-length plays.

An examination of the background against which the plays are set shows not so much a predominance of historical settings as of rural ones, whether the Highlands, the Lowlands or the Southern Uplands. The dramatists seem to have gone to great lengths to avoid contemporary urban settings, although they apparently felt quite at home in the countryside. Of the twenty-one most performed plays, leaving aside *The Late Christopher Bean* (a non-Scots play performed late in the Players' career), it can be said that five are historical plays. (*Clyde-Built* is a possible sixth candidate, but is set close enough to the time of writing to be considered non-historical). Of these plays *The Walls of Jericho* is set in the Edinburgh of 1843 while *The Dawn*, *Campbell of Kilmohr*, *The Mother* and *The Scarecrow* are set in the Highlands. *The Dawn* and *Campbell of Kilmohr* are set in the aftermath of the Jacobite troubles, *The Mother* during the Clearances and *The Scarecrow* in Inverness-shire during the early nineteenth century. Most of the five historical plays are remote both in time and place.

Of the remaining sixteen plays almost all are set in rural surroundings, the Highlands in the case of *The Glen is Mine*, most of *The Flower in the Vase* and *The Grenadier*, and elsewhere in Scotland in the case of the others. The only exceptions are *S. for Sugar Candy*, the light comedy about a sweet factory, *Clyde-Built* and *C'Est La Guerre*, which is set in France during the First World War.

We have here more evidence of the phenomenon, already remarked upon, of dramatists choosing not the industrial urban society with which they and their audiences were most familiar, but writing instead either about the past or about rural society. These dramatists, it would seem, felt much surer of themselves when they were not dealing with first-hand experience. They preferred to shy away from the problems of identity which the contemporary world confronted them with, and to extend the kailyard view of Scottish experience.

This is not true of all the plays. Joe Corrie's, for all their rural background, are set on the fringes of urban society and deal with situations which are found in such a society; George Blake writes about the Clyde; but these are the exceptions. Glasgow, where all the theatrical activity was taking place, scarcely makes an appearance, and the First World War, the effects of which were far from remote during this period, is hardly dealt with at all.

There is throughout the work we have been looking at an obsession with the Highlands. This is, of course, one aspect of the Scottish search for identity. Highland experience is markedly different from life in the rest of the British Isles; therefore if the Scot can see himself as a Highlander he has found a distinctive identity that is not open to him as a Lowlander. It is not, however, the case that the view of the Highlands put forward in these plays is consistently a romantic, nostalgic or escapist one. True, there are pieces like Naomi Jacob's *The Dawn* and Brandane's largely comic view of the Highlands, which is at times of dubious validity. On the other hand, there are the grim realities of the Highlands, past and present, to be found in J. A. Ferguson's work and Malloch's *The Grenadier*, and Brandane in *The Glen is Mine* does attempt to deal with contemporary Highland problems.

Where the real failure comes is in the plays concerned with the rest of Scotland, which is seen as a rural backwater totally unaffected by the twentieth century. What is worse, it is only rarely that there is any penetration below the surface of rural life. Obviously, we cannot expect this of light-hearted comedies, but we could do with more plays like *The Mannoch Family* and *Soutarness Water*, which, whatever their deficiencies, convey a sense of real experience. Bridie's plays performed by the Players are really the exception that proves the rule in this case. His interest in contemporary Glasgow mores was not generally shared by his fellow dramatists. Nor were his plays very popular with the Players' audiences.

One problem, in which these writers avoided being submerged, was that of language. The renaissance in Scottish poetry this century was bedevilled by arguments as to whether to write in English or Lallans or some other form of Scots. The problem was not likely to be so acute in the drama for the simple reason that it is a convention of the naturalistic theatre that the characters speak for the most part in a fashion that is approximately like that used by their real-life counterparts. As many of the plays we have discussed are naturalistic in form and set in areas where dialect was still spoken at the time of writing, it was possible to use the Scots of the particular area, and this may be another reason why dramatists preferred rural settings: they were able to use Scots without producing the uneasy situation where contemporary characters speak in archaic language. The rural setting, because dialect could be employed, possibly seemed to them to be that much more Scottish than the urban one, although there was nothing to prevent a writer from rendering the Glasgow dialect on the stage, as Unity's writers were later to do.

Casting one's mind finally over the plays performed by the Scottish National Players one remembers a few plays of considerable merit and rather a large number of mediocre ones. However this is all we can expect from a drama which, it cannot be emphasized too often, was only beginning and has yet to come to full fruition.

CHAPTER SEVEN

The Achievements of the Players

IN ASSESSING THE WORK of the Scottish National Players, we must immediately give credit for their sustained efforts to cultivate an exclusively Scottish drama. It is easy to condemn them for the non-appearance of large numbers of outstanding plays — it is difficult to ascertain to what extent they were to blame — but we must admire their determination, as we must also admire the way in which they sought to turn their movement into a national one. It is easy also to make fun of the camping tours, but in a country which has no substantial dramatic tradition, and which was scarcely flourishing when these tours took place, they were a brave attempt to educate an audience for Scottish theatre. Critics remarked at the time on the excellent work the Players undertook in promoting drama outside the urban areas and in stimulating higher standards of amateur activity. The Players may well have shown rural drama clubs how to act, but unfortunately they did not interest them greatly in good plays, for they did not have many to display.

Much contemporary comment — in the *Scottish Stage* for example — is hostile to the Players' policy in the selection of plays. In that periodical in May 1933 there appeared a letter by Murray McClymont entitled Have the S.N.P. failed?, in which McClymont said that he had received a letter from the Players asking for a play from him, adding that they felt let down by Scottish dramatists. McClymont disagreed violently and criticised the Players for seeking to "perpetuate the hoary tradition of glens and pipers, of kail and kitchens". The Players, said McClymont, would only gain the support of Scottish writers when they attempted to create a Scottish theatre. So far they had done nothing for Scottish theatrical art. He went on to make the rather strange point that the Players were "content to figure as a branch of the English theatre", a remark suggesting that not all criticism of the Players was consistent or fair.

It is however interesting to note that McClymont's condemnation of the Players' supposed predilections for plays that bore little relation to the life of Scotland was very similar to some of the criticism made against the amateur movement in general. This is to be expected since, as has been emphasized, the Players were basically part of the amateur movement. Other criticisms made at the time were: their choice of plays favoured the mediocre and the parochial; they took far too long to read and comment on scripts submitted; they dissipated their energies on Highland tours. It is difficult to evaluate these criticisms. The evidence we have consists of the plays actually presented, the company's declarations of policy, the criticisms themselves and revealing incidents such as the agonies which the Players seem to have undergone in deciding whether to stage G. R. Malloch's *Soutarness Water*.

The real trouble with the Scottish National Players was not that they took a long time to make up their minds about scripts or were squeamish about particular plays, but that few of the plays they put on reflected accurately the contemporary social background, and fewer still were of any lasting merit. The awkward question still arises, however — did the Players actively prevent the growth of a genuine and truthful Scottish drama?

Few writers were in any doubt about the lack of a Scottish drama. As Dot Allan commented in 1924, "Scotland alone of European countries has no real drama of its own". Many reasons were given for the lack of a Scottish theatre — the Puritan tradition was a favourite, the lack of a national theatre building was frequently mentioned (Tyrone Guthrie blamed the failure of the Scottish National Players partly on the lack of a suitable permanent building), as was the loss of independence. Writing in *Scottish Stage* in 1932, Murray McClymont declared that "theatrically, we are, and have been for over four hundred years, a conquered nation". Our theatre, he argued with some justice, is highly dependent on England's. Extending McClymont's point, it can be suggested that the growth and popularity of the Kailyard School was due to a crisis in the Scottish identity. When Scotland ceased to be an independent country, Scottishness was asserted by emphasizing those aspects of Scottish life obviously different from the life of England. At the same time nostalgia for a lost identity and a desire to escape from the industrial milieu led writers into treating these aspects in a dishonest, sentimental fashion.

Neil Gunn sympathized with the views alluded to above, but remained sceptical. We cannot, he wrote, in the *Scots Magazine* (December 1938), expect a drama like the Irish one, because there had been no source of national conflict or travail out of which great drama grows. A national theatre will serve no purpose if there is nothing to express. Great dramatic writing springs from a vigorous national life, and this cannot be guaranteed either by building national theatres, setting up academies and cultural committees or declaring independence. It is something which is either there or it is not; and only when it is can dramatists take advantage of it. It does not, of course, follow that if there is no great conflict or trauma in a nation's affairs that there is nothing to write about. Dramatists can still write plays which accurately reflect the life of the people in the nation or region — post-war English drama after all has to an extent been regional drama. Hopes were expressed that such plays would be forthcoming by, for example, Marion Lochhead, who looked to "the wonder and poetry of the Celt", free from sentimentality and mysticism, to produce great drama, possibly an Aeschylean tragedy.

The problem resolved itself into one of definition — what could be distinctively Scottish in the drama? As MacDiarmid's *Northern Review* put it:

> *It has been a criticism pertinently levelled at Scots drama so far that it has found no distinctive form, but manifests itself simply as provincial variations on the established forms of the British stage. It does not reflect fundamentally, whatever it may do superficially, the profound differences in psychology between Scots and English.* (May 1924)

Some writers were of the opinion that this was a matter of technique. Notable among theorists of a Scottish theatrical technique was R. F. Pollock who worked with the Dumbarton People's Theatre and other amateur companies. The Scot's characteristics, said Pollock, are intensity and brevity: he feels a great deal but does not express himself volubly; he is imaginative, analytic, individual, starkly realistic, utterly independent and highly self-conscious. All this, not surprisingly, cannot be conveyed, in terms of the conventional theatre:

> *The form of drama he could therefore understand and enjoy would be more a commentary on an action, just like the ballad, than an episodic account of an action. Dialogue would be directed towards revealing psychological truth,*

rather than recounting incident. The aim would be to
portray thoughts and feelings, rather than episodes and
actions.   (Scots Magazine, November 1930)

What Pollock — obviously influenced by Stanislawski —
appears to be saying is that Scottish speech is indicative of much
more below the surface than is the case with other nationalities,
and that this characteristic is fundamental to a native theatrical
technique. He refers particularly to the Scot's use of mono-
syllables and emphasizes that an actor needs a particular
approach to convey the full force of their meaning on the stage.
Pollock is right to insist on the peculiar qualities of Scottish
expression, but these of course could only be properly exploited
in a play suitable for the purpose, in the same way that
Stanislawski's methods were only really of use with a particular
type of drama, the poetic naturalism of Chekhov. Without plays
which call for it a Scottish technique as advocated by Pollock is
of no use, indeed it is a handicap.

Many commentators, a large number of whom were themselves playwrights, discussed the types of play they should like to
see on the Scottish stage: themes such as the Clearances, the
slum problem and various other industrial subjects were
suggested. Jack House, writing in *Scottish Stage* (May 1936),
argued that a theatre of the Left was necessary in Scotland. It is
very important to realise, and possibly crucial, that not everyone
was in favour of the type of play suggested by the writers whose
views have just been alluded to. The opinions of Hal D. Stewart,
a kind of anti-highbrow crusader in the Scottish National Players,
were frequently published. In November 1932 he had written that
"Too many contributors have already sought to point the
amateur to the highbrow path. I will not add to this number".
Stewart's battle cry was taken up. Gordon Wright declared that
he was quite happy with kitchen comedy and referred to the
"highbrow yelp for 'serious contributions to the theatre'."
(*Scottish Stage*, December 1936)

We must beware of exaggerating the importance of Stewart
and those of like mind, but nevertheless they probably represented a considerable body of opinion in the amateur movement
as a whole and a vocal secion of opinion in the Scottish National
Players, and indeed their voice can still be heard loud and clear
in the land. It does not follow that this body of opinion in the

Players prevented the growth of a serious Scottish drama, but its presence is bound to have discouraged potential dramatists who may have felt that light, undemanding plays were preferred to anything more ambitious. Beyond this unsatisfactory conclusion — on the available evidence — we cannot go.

On the positive side we should not forget, in considering the work of the Players and the amateur movement of which it was a part, that it did serve as a training ground for Scottish actors, something which was badly needed in the days before the College of Drama was established. The Players did a rather different job from the College since, as they were presenting mainly Scottish plays, their actors needed to develop a style suitable to the material. The Drama College on the other hand has to train its actors with both the English and Scottish stages and also television in mind.

Enquiries among surviving members of the Players regarding acting style have not produced very definite conclusions. Some cannot remember anything peculiarly Scottish about the acting style, while one member feels that the styles used in Highland plays and Lowland comedy were distinctively Scottish. The style in the former, he feels, was similar to that employed in the Abbey Theatre, while in Lowland comedy a Truth to Nature style was used. This last comment, read alongside remarks made by others of the Players, leads one to conclude that in Scottish plays there was employed a naturalism which differed from what one might find in, say, English or Russian plays performed on the native stage. The explanation lies more in the generalization that the English and Russian peoples are different in such things as gesture and intonation than in any deliberate attempt on the part of the Players to cultivate a distinctive style of acting. It is more likely that the prevailing style of naturalism was adjusted to suit the material.

What the Players did towards developing a pool of acting talent in Scotland should not be belittled. There can be no national drama unless there are actors geared to presenting it. Although the Players' actors were trained on largely mediocre material, that training could have been put to good use in plays of merit, as it has been since, not least on the several occasions when a Scottish cast, including many former members of the Players and the other groups such as the Curtain Theatre, presented Sir David Lindsay's *The Three Estates* at the Edinburgh Festival. Actors like James Gibson, Grace McChlery and Jean Taylor Smith began with the Players.

It is not proposed to embark on an extensive consideration of why the Scottish National Players ultimately ceased to exist. The difficult theatrical situation, which was discussed in the chapter on the Glasgow Repertory Company, still prevailed when the Players were operating, and they suffered the consequences. Perhaps if they had turned professional or had had a permanent home in Glasgow they might have survived longer. Better plays might have helped — or they might regrettably have had the opposite effect! In the end, however, the Players would have probably gone under like every other non-commercial theatre in Scotland unfortunate enough to have been alive before the era of subsidy began. Also, in a sense they had the worst of both worlds: they lacked the local support amateur companies command in small communities, but they also lacked the financial and artistic resources which the professional theatre deploys to attract customers.

As with the Glasgow Repertory venture, a study of the reports of the AGMs of the Scottish National Players shows optimism and enthusiasm waning as support and financial backing do not come up to expectation. At the 1922 AGM it was stated that the membership of the society was 835 which was not considered high enough (by 1925 this figure had reached 1,026 but two years later it had dropped again to 820). A loss of £176 had been sustained on the year's working, and it was said that:

> If there were 500 additional persons per performance they
> would be able to show a profit . . . and enable them to
> stage historical and costume plays.   (Glasgow Herald, 28
> December 1922)

Despite the unrosy outlook, it was decided to embark on an auxiliary productions scheme whereby members of the Society could have their plays performed at private meetings and dissected afterwards by the other members present. Several sessions under the auspices of this excellent scheme seem to have been held.

At the 1925 AGM the chairman expressed satisfaction at the year's work, which included broadcasts, but was faced with a loss of £140. However, he was able to announce that the building fund which had been started a few years previously, had received a boost through a donation of £500 (the fund however never exceeded £620). At the 1926 AGM it was proposed to establish a guarantee fund since with another loss, this time of £138, the production fund stood at £212, and the following year it was reported at the AGM that 18/11½ in the pound of the guarantee fund for *James the First of Scotland* had had to be called up. In 1929 the loss on the previous year's working had reached £449 and in 1930 £788. When it was decided to suspend operations in 1934, it was stated that the society had been formally constitued in 1928 with capital of £4000 (when the limited liability company was founded in 1928 to further the objects of the Players it was registered with capital of £10,000 but only 4000 shares were taken up), but as a result of losses each year this had been whittled down to £400. It was pointed out that most of the losses were sustained in the towns and not in the rural areas. The directors hoped that it would be possible for some of the company's work to continue, if only in offering guidance to aspiring playwrights.

The company did not in fact disband but insisted on carrying on, which it did until the War, and it finally petered out in 1947. The programming policy was changed after the formal suspension of operations towards a greater reliance on light comedies, many of which originated in the English professional theatre, and the Scottish content of the programme diminished. The Players ceased to be "Scottish National" in the sense that they no longer adhered to the original aims. The initiative in the presentation of new Scottish plays had passed to The Curtain.

As for the achievements of the drama compared to those of the novel and poetry during the Scottish renaissance, it will probably be clear to the reader that they are less substantial. This is hardly surprising in view of the poor base from which drama was starting. And while it would be agreeable to be able to point to dramatists whose achievement was equal to that of the novelist Neil Gunn or the poet Hugh MacDiarmid, a sense of realism must tell us that it was too soon to expect such maturity in the drama during the period under discussion. However there was one playwright, who began to have his work performed in the years between the wars, for whom substantial claims can be made; and it is to him that we now turn our attention.

A 19th-century playhouse — the Theatre Royal, Dunlop Street, Glasgow, demolished in 1869 (*T. & R. Annan*)

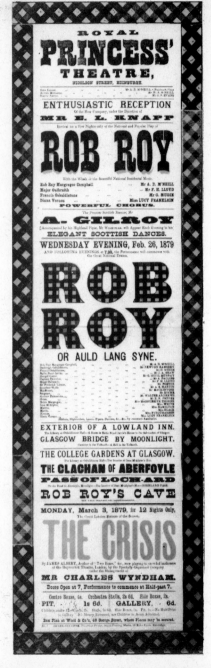

Playbill for an Edinburgh production of *Rob Roy* in 1879 (*Edinburgh City Libraries*)

Some founding figures in the history of Scottish theatre: top left — Alfred Wareing: top right — John Stewart (*Pitlochry Festival Theatre*); lower left — Glen McKemmie; lower right — Marjorie Dence (*Perth Repertory Theatre*)

James Bridie and the Citizens' Theatre in 1947   (*Glasgow Citizens' Theatre*)

Portraits of four playwrights: top left — John Bradane (*Glasgow Herald*); top right — Robert McLellan (*J. M. Forgie*); lower left — Robert Kemp (*Stephens Orr*); lower right — Cecil Taylor (*George Oliver*)

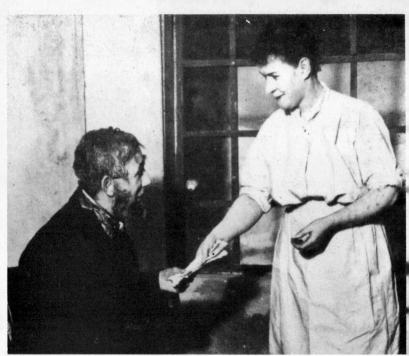

A Scottish National Players production of *The Glen is Mine* with Archie Buchanan and Nell Ballantyne; and an early summer camping tour under the leadership of Tyrone Guthrie (extreme right)

Top — a scene from the 1950 Edinburgh Festival production by Glasgow Citizens' of James Bridie's *The Queen's Comedy* with Sonia Dresdel as Juno and Stanley Baxter as Mercury; **bottom** — Duncan Macrae rehearsing with members of Glasgow Citizens' for their 1947 production of Robert McLellan's *Jamie the Saxt* (*Glasgow Citizens' Theatre*)

Left — Cecil Taylor's *Bread and Butter* from the 1969 Traverse production with Maggie Jordan, Michael Harrigan, Eileen Nicholas and Peter Lincoln (*Diane Tammes*); right — Ron Bain in Dundee Repertory Theatre's 1971 production of George Munro's *Mark But This Flea* (*Alec Cooper, Span Photo*)

CHAPTER EIGHT
James Bridie

ANY ACCOUNT OF THE SCOTTISH THEATRE must of necessity deal with the contribution of Osborne Henry Mavor (1888-1951) who wrote under the pen-name of James Bridie. Bridie's contribution was twofold — his plays, and his untiring work to establish the theatre firmly in Scotland.

Bridie, by far the most distinguished man of the theatre that Scotland has produced, was born into a respectable and reasonably prosperous Glasgow family, his father being an engineer. He was educated at Glasgow Academy (appearing to have suffered there the tribulations that attend the non-athletic boy) and at Glasgow University, where he graduated in medicine. Apart from a period of war service, which took him to the East, he spent the rest of his life in Glasgow or in the surrounding area. Although in his early years he was not without financial worries, success came to him as a doctor with his appointment as a consultant at a Glasgow hospital. It also came to him as a playwright, for which career he was able eventually to abandon medicine.

Bridie's interest in the theatre had been stimulated by what he had seen in Glasgow as a young man and in particular the seasons mounted by the Glasgow Repertory Company under Alfred Wareing. Bridie time after time won competitions run by Wareing and the Glasgow press for the best critical reviews of the Royalty productions; Wareing then invited Bridie to write a play for the theatre but unfortunately illness intervened and Bridie found himself companion to Wareing while the latter convalesced in the Highlands. The play was ultimately completed but was never put on, and subsequently lost. After the First World War Bridie turned to writing again and sent *The Switchback* to Wareing who was now in Huddersfield. Wareing commented that the play was too clever for any manager to present (in fact, it was presented by Sir Barry Jackson at Birmingham in 1929). Some years after its formation Bridie joined the board of the Scottish National Players and he was one of the directors most determined that the Players should turn professional. When the Players chose not to do so Bridie left the

Board, since he felt that the policy being pursued was disastrous.

It is when we come to the formation of the Citizens' Theatre in Glasgow during the Second World War that we reach the period in Bridie's life when he made the greatest contribution to the development of the Scottish theatre. He was chairman of the Citizens' from its inception until his death; he played the major role in establishing the College of Drama in Glasgow in 1950 as an extension of the Royal Scottish Academy of Music; he was a member of the Arts Council and at one point Scottish chairman; he was adviser on drama to the Edinburgh Festival.

Bridie's contribution to nurturing the theatre in Scotland was matched by a substantial output of dramatic works. It would be foolish to pretend that every one of his plays has something of very great importance to say. He was, as he often emphasized, an entertainer, diverting an audience for a couple of hours:

> *A play is a method of passing an interval of time. A stage play is a method of passing an interval of time by putting an actor or actors on a platform and causing them to say or do certain things. If it is amusing, that is to say if it succeeds in making the spectators unconscious of the passing of time, it fulfils its function and has merit. If, on the other hand, the spectators are conscious of the passing of time, of the dreadful progress of the Universe towards destruction and nothingness, the play has failed and has no merit, or at least, no merit as a play. Other qualities of a play — its educative, its thought-provoking, its exciting, its poetic qualities — are not basic.* (Tedious and Brief, London 1944)

We can see here Bridie's emphasis on the theatrical aspect of drama. He did not however regard the theatre as a "mean or frivolous activity", but took the view that a play makes us believe we are participating in a fuller life than the one we actually endure. It would be foolish to accept Bridie's own judgement of himself as a mere entertainer, although it should be stressed that as a dramatist he is extremely conscious of the need to keep the audience interested. Many of his plays do comment on human experience at the same time as they divert or amuse. But his constant reluctance to make any very substantial claims for his work is important, and it can be argued that this was Bridie's way of protecting himself against a society whose response to artists is indifference or derision. As Christopher Small has commented:

> *no one is more exposed to the uncomprehending laughter of his fellows than the artist, and nowhere more, perhaps, than in the solidly, one may say almost impenetrably Philistine society of middle-class Glasgow when Bridie was young. He was an artist, he couldn't help it; but he could ward off laughter by getting his laugh in first, both at others and at himself.* (Scottish Theatre, January 1971)

The theme which recurs constantly in Bridie's work — it is almost a moral — can be stated quite simply: man as a species should accept his cosmic limitations and individual men should accept their personal shortcomings. One can easily see how a society which derides claims to anything better than the humdrum produces this attitude in a writer. In a sense it is a reflection of that society's own attitude, but it is also a refuge for the exposed artist that Bridie felt himself to be.

Acceptance of one's limitations can be a very dispiriting philosophy and Bridie would appear to have been dissatisfied with it, for in many of his plays he tries a little too hard to justify such a world view, sometimes with the help of divine intervention! The corollary seems to be that the not particularly significant man — the man who does not have what would be regarded as pretensions — is a man to be rated as highly as the greatest and most spectacular of men. In these plays Bridie is not merely concerned with particular characters, he is reflecting something of himself and his own reluctance, even fear, to go too far, to attempt the grandiose or magnificent. This theme in Bridie's work derives very largely from middle-class Glasgow and indeed middle-class Scotland. In some ways it is the most Scottish thing about him.

In three of his plays with Biblical background, *Tobias and the Angel*, *Jonah and the Whale* and *Susannah and the Elders*, Bridie concentrates his attention on the limitations of the human species. *Tobias and the Angel* (20 November 1930, Cambridge Festival Theatre) is based on the Apocryphal Book of Tobit, and tells with considerable wit the story of Tobias, son of the blind Tobit, who travels to Hamadan accompanied by a servant Azarias (who is the archangel Gabriel in disguise). After surviving, with Azarias's help, several dire perils including an encounter with a devil called Asmody, Tobias marries a wealthy girl, Sara. On Tobias's return to Nineveh, Raphael/Azarias restores old Tobit's sight, and all look set to live happily ever after, although in Sara's case acceptance of her lot has only come after a struggle. She has fallen in love with Raphael to whom she insists that she has grown impatient with the ordinary run of men; she prefers Raphael of whose real identity she is well aware. Raphael tells her to treat him as Tobias's spirit or daemon, and refuses to listen to her as she pleads that she is dissatisfied with ordinary mortals:

> You must cease to be so. Often at odd times in the future, you will see me looking out of Tobias's eyes. But you must look the other way and busy yourself with your household tasks.

Jonah and the Whale (12 December 1932, Westminster Theatre, London), a slighter play, is a retelling of the Jonah story in a witty fashion, with a large number of contemporary allusions — a style of writing at which Bridie is particularly adept. He appears to regard Jonah as a baleful Puritan influence of whom the people of Gitta-Hepher are well rid. Jonah is no sooner outside the city gate than drinking, singing and dancing break out again within the walls. In the play Jonah is brought to realize, when Nineveh is not destroyed, "I am only an ordinary man".

The moral is more specific in *Susannah and the Elders* (31 October 1937, Duke of York's Theatre, London). Man is highly fallible and, when he falls, should not be spurned but pitied.

As Bridie explains in the preface, in his adaptation of the Apocryphal story he has placed the emphasis on the elders, for whom he has a great deal of sympathy. They seem to him to represent a kind of person and a kind of failure, which are common:

> *Every now and then some distinguished old man, a*
> *respected and wise servant of his country and mankind,*
> *does some silly and outrageous act that gets his name into*
> *the police-court records and the sniggering sort of Sunday*
> *newspaper.*
> *Most of us turn away our heads from this heartbreaking*
> *thing; but it is as right a topic for a goat-song as jealousy,*

revenge or any other kind of ignominy, that soils without
destroying the nobility of man.

Before the play opens, a Reader, dressed as a kind of Court
official, sets the scene and enlists our sympathy for the elders
before the action itself begins:

> The old story says that these Judges who did this
> wickedness were false and evil to the bone; but who knows
> the heart of a man and what moves in that darkness? And
> is there any man living who has in him no tincture of
> goodness, however unhappily he may do in his life?
> Tonight you are to be the judges of these old Judges.
> Search yourselves well that you may do justly.

It is therefore clear that this will not be a play where we are
confronted with black and white moral situations, but with those
of finer shades of grey.

The opening scenes demonstrate the harshness and
inflexibility of Babylonian law, and the dramatist obviously feels
that such laws fail to take account of the human weakness with
which he is concerned in the play. The elders themselves,
Kashdak and Kabbittu, are presented as sympathetic characters
whose weakness is common to mankind. All men, Bridie seems
to be saying, put on a front of respectability and morality, but
beneath this front most of them have something to hide. The
mistake the elders make is that they forget that beneath their
respectable ageing exteriors the force of lust is still smouldering.
As they discover all too painfully, they have mistaken the form
for the reality. This indeed is one of the central themes of the
play, the contrast between appearance and reality. During his
trial on a charge on blasphemy Dionysos, a Greek, insists to
Kabbittu who is sitting on the bench, that judges no more
believe in the gods he has blasphemed against than he does:

> KABBITTU: That is beside the point. My duty as a law
> giver is to give the gods the benefit of the doubt. It is
> true that within the walls of this city, we are not
> particularly enthusiastic about the gods. But we have a
> very distinct impression . . . a very persistent idea that if
> we don't treat them with some respect they will go out
> into the desert and become evil spirits. I don't know
> whether you have much experience of the desert . . .

DIONYSOS: I have, your worship.

KABBITTU: You will know, then, that it is a very
different matter out there, where there are no lighted
shops and no policemen! It is not pleasant, Dionysos, to
have a bad-tempered demon trampling on one's shadow.

DIONYSOS: No.

KABBITTU: The desert is crowded with them as it is. At
night they come pressing in against our walls. So we build,
for those who remain in the city, nice temples with cosy
altars. And we insist that our citizens and our guests
treat them properly. Does that seem to you reasonable?

DIONYSOS: Very reasonable, your worship.

What Kabbittu appears to be saying here is that if the
forms are observed, then life will proceed in an orderly fashion
and, in the case of the judges themselves, in an urbane and
civilized fashion. There is of course an ironic contrast between
this graceful living and the savage Babylonian penal system. The
further irony is that the judges are soon to place themselves in a
position of the most base hypocrisy, so attracted are they to the
beautiful young Susannah. There are hints, as the play
progresses, that they are beginning to sense the gap between
appearance and reality, but that does not prevent the catastrophe.
Lust and hypocrisy combine to bring about their downfall.
Exposed, they accept their fate with resignation. In his last
speech before judgement is delivered Kabbittu admits his false-
seeming:

All the world has known me as a kindly, just, respectable
man. And so I thought myself. For I forgot how the exalted
Anu had made us all. What you saw was the head of a
man, uttering discreet things, above the robes of a grave
and seemly magistrate. Beneath these robes was the body
of a goat. The head ensures and cherishes honour, justice,
pity, shame and a good conscience; the beast can be
tamed, but he knows nothing of any of these things.

It is not at all surprising that Bridie should choose to
concentrate — albeit sympathetically — on the hypocrisy of the
elders; for hypocrisy, while not peculiarly Scottish, is considered
a characteristic of our life and a major concern of our literature.
Lindsay was concerned with it in *The Three Estates*, Burns in,
for example, *Holy Willie's Prayer* and several of the dramatists

dealt with in this book return to it as a theme. The contrast between actuality and seeming is found also, in slightly different form, in Stevenson (*Dr Jekyll and Mr Hyde*, *Weir of Hermiston*) and Hogg (*Confessions of a Justified Sinner*), where the concern is not merely with hypocrisy but dual personality.

Susannah herself is not presented as a paradigm of innocence. She is in fact a mixture of characteristics. Her maids find her a bit straightlaced and when Dionysos, the appropriately-named Greek who constantly makes passes at her, talks of the orgies in Corinth, she declares herself disgusted. On the other hand, at one point she tells her mother-in-law:

> I'd like to get into bad company myself, just once, for a change. It must be very interesting!

It is certainly this side of Susannah which attracts Dionysos and, for that matter, partially accounts for the elders' feelings.

Susannah and the Elders, to sum up, is a play of considerable depth where, despite an anti-climactic final court scene, the dramatic power and the theme with which Bridie is concerned combine to sustain the audience's interest and involve them emotionally without the distortion of sentimentality.

Daphne Laureola (23 March 1949, Wyndham's Theatre, London), Bridie's most commercially successful play, is similar in theme to the three biblical plays discussed above, although the action is set in the modern period. It relates the infatuation of Ernest Piaste, a romantic young man, for Lady Pitts — an infatuation which is not shared by her ladyship who, on her husband's death, marries her chauffeur. Ernest protests that this has shattered his dream of her:

> Has nobody told you the story of the poor peasant who worshipped a goddess? And then he found there were no gods and goddesses, only an empty sky?

Lady Pitts refuses to be impressed by this talk of despair and tells Ernest that she has merely served as a vehicle onto which he has projected his illusions:

> It never occurred to him that I was a human being. They're all the same — unless they're pigs. And the pigs are at least honest with themselves and with us. I've found that out now. That's why I've settled down in a nice clean pig-sty.

The lot which human beings have to accept in this play is gloomier than that of Sara in *Tobias and the Angel* but the basic message is much the same, though Bridie is here suggesting, as he has not done before, that dreams and fantasies are idle follies which can quickly turn sour.

Several of Bridie's plays are concerned with the personal and environmental limitations of particular men, rather than with the limitations of mankind in general. *The Switchback*, *Colonel Wotherspoon*, *Babes in the Wood* and *The Golden Legend of Shults* centre on such limitations. They are all amusing if dated comedies.

The best expression of Bridie's feelings about the worth of the small man, another aspect of his basic theme, is to be found in *Mr Gillie* (13 February 1950, King's Theatre, Glasgow). Mr Gillie — a part originally created on the stage by Alastair Sim with whom Bridie had a long and close working relationship — is a village schoolmaster on the west coast of Scotland. A failed man of letters himself, he has nonetheless encouraged many young people to trust the talents he discerns in them, only to see them come to grief in the outside world or prostitute their talents, as he would have it. The play is set within a heavenly framework in which the Procurator and the Judge are discussing whither it would be appropriate to consign Mr Gillie, who has died after being knocked down by a pantechnicon. The Judge, ignoring the Procurator's insistence that Gillie's life was a useless one, places him between Lincoln and John Wesley. "Let us honour the forlorn hope", declares the Judge: the small man's obscure life, even when apparently a failure, can nonetheless be regarded as being as significant as other lives lived in the midst of public acclaim.

Bridie's championing of the ordinary man's integrity and importance, and his implication that small men (i.e. most of us in the average audience) should content themselves with their lot, has another side to it. This is a somewhat ambivalent admiration for super-men figures who tend to over-ride, apparently with Bridie's approval, the ordinary demands of decency and morality. As ordinary men in an audience are consoled by a dramatist assuring them that they matter, so they respond sympathetically to the depiction of men completely free from the bonds of propriety that so restrain them.

The Anatomist (6 July 1930, Masque Theatre in Royal

Lyceum) is a historical play based on the Burke and Hare case, and it centres its attention on Doctor Knox, the recipient of the body-snatchers' victims. Knox is presented as a man with contempt for lesser mortals, so dedicated to what he sees as the truth that he is apparently unconcerned when told that one of his anatomical subjects may have been murdered:

> The life of this poor wretch is ended. It is surely a better thing that her beauty of form should be at the service of divine science than at the services of any drunken buck with a crown in his pocket.

Even when he relents somewhat, Knox is determined that he shall be answerable only to God. He is above trafficking with ordinary human beings when it comes to discussing the morality of his conduct, for all his occasional sentimental lapses. Although Bridie does not explicitly indicate his agreement with Knox's attitude, there can be little doubt that he has some sympathy for it. At the end of the play he leaves us with a picture of Knox, having triumphed over the mob which threatened to lynch him, lecturing in his usual assertive, domineering manner.

A Sleeping Clergyman (29 July 1933, Malvern Festival), another medical play, tells the story of the generations in the Cameron family, and spans the period from the 1860s to the 1930s. Charlie Cameron the first is a medical student in Glasgow, much admired by Joseph Lister, but an unpleasant young man nonetheless. He behaves abominably to his landlady and friends and only agrees to marry a girl who is pregnant by him when he knows he is dying. The redeeming feature in Cameron's character is the spark of genius which only grows to fruition in his grandson. Genius, it appears, is above the ordinary laws of decency and morality.

There co-exist in the characters of Cameron's descendants genius and amorality. His daughter flirts with a servant then casts him off when a richer catch presents itself. When the servant threatens to show her prospective husband the letters he has received from her, she poisons him with prussic acid (a detail that owes something to the famous Madeleine Smith murder case). Her son, Charlie Sutherland, has the same disregard for others that his mother and grandfather showed. For example, during the First World War, when he should have been at a family reunion that had been arranged for his benefit, he spends the night with a prostitute in London. But twenty years after this he is in charge of a research establishment at the height of an epidemic which is threatening London and the world. The vaccine that he has developed works and the world is saved! Hence, Bridie seems to be suggesting, the boorish and amoral behaviour of Charlie and his family is justifiable for they have genius.

If we consider other aspects of Bridie's work we discover the scant attention given to the essentially Scottish conflict between the precepts of Calvinism and the natural impulses of life. *John Knox*, the play in which one might expect that conflict to be examined, is a reconstruction of history whose chief interest is the presentation of the action as a series of flashbacks from modern times.

Mr Bolfry (8 August 1943, Westminster Theatre, London), the one play in which Bridie does seriously attempt to come to grips with Calvinism, is set in the Free Kirk Manse at Larach in the West Highlands during the war. Two English soldiers, Cully and Cohen, are billeted here and are bemoaning the rigours of a Presbyterian Sunday. Jean Ogilvie, niece of the Rev. Mr McCrimmon, puts in an appearance and Cohen's spirits rise considerably. They decide to take on her uncle in philosophical debate later in the day. Jean is a young lady who takes a very cynical view of Calvinist pretensions to morality. Of the parish she says, "It's got the best record for church attendance and the highest illegitimacy rate in the Kingdom", and of the parishioners:

They stick to hedges and ditches for their special
occasions. Disgusting, superstitious pigs. And they're not
only immoral and hypocritical. They're Devil-Worshippers.

The theme of the play has thus been introduced. What is the true nature of Presbyterian Calvinism? Is it the worship of God or of the devil? Bridie's answer, as we shall see, seems to be that in the heart of Calvinism there is a repression which stems from a refusal to acknowledge the darkness within. Calvinism, for Jean is a deadly religion. As she says, "It kills everything that's gay and decent in life".

The debate between Jean and Mr McCrimmon continues on a supernatural level when Mr Bolfry, an emissary of the devil but dressed like a minister, is conjured up. Bolfry, an extremely amiable and smooth character, insists on the necessity of the devil and hell:

> To put it in simple words we cannot conceive the Universe except as a pattern of reciprocating opposites. Therefore, when I tell you that there are kirks in Hell, I am telling you something that is at least credible.

Mr McCrimmon attempts to refute Bolfry's argument, but to little effect. However, shortly after this, when Cohen announces that he is bored stiff by all the argy-bargy, Bolfry and McCrimmon team up in an attempt to save the souls of Cohen and the others, and to convince them that there is a purpose in the universe. Bolfry goes on to preach a sermon. At first he extends the eminently reasonable argument put by him earlier that good and evil are necessary conflicting opposites. Soon, however, it becomes clear that such urbanity is a mask for the forces of darkness, and Bolfry goes on to claim that he represents these very forces which seek to overthrow those of good and that once they have done so, "Man's genius will burst its bonds and leap to meet the sun":

> My flags are the Pride of the Eye and the Lust of the Flesh. Their other names are Art and Poetry, and where they wave the abomination of desolation can never be. How long, O Lucifer, Son of the Morning, how long? How long will these fools listen to the quaverings of impotent old priests, haters of the life they never know? How long will they saddle their strong limbs in dusty parchments? How long will they shut out the sky from their eyes with prisons of cold stone? I tell you that all you have and all you know is your Self. Honour your Self and set him free; for the Soul and the Body are one, and their only home is the World, and their only life is the Flesh and their only friend is the Devil. Let the wild horses loose!

There is unhappily a certain confusion in the play. Bolfry on the one hand can be taken to represent evil (he in fact claims to have started the war), but on the other he appears to be stating traditional anti-Puritan arguments. Yet again, he is dressed as a minister and claims to have been ordained, he can be taken to represent Calvinism in essence. The confusion arises because Bridie seems to be in two minds as to what he is trying to do, and so Bolfry has to fill several roles. He has to be the attractive devil (as in *Tam O'Shanter*) who represents the honest pleasures of the world which the life-denying Puritans spurn. He has also to be the unattractive devil, representing not honest pleasure but pure evil, whilst at the same time becoming an embodiment of the repressive side of Puritanism. It is too much to expect a character to fulfil such conflicting roles and it is a pity that Bridie could not have resolved this conflict before writing the play. As it is, Bolfry acts out the role of unattractive devil, representing the evil that is in man's heart. McCrimmon recognizes this, announces that he will extirpate the voice of evil and symbolically chases Bolfry from his house with a knife. Bolfry leaps over a cliff to his death. The next morning all concerned discuss the bad dreams they have had, and are on the point of dismissing them when Bolfry's umbrella, which he has left behind, walks out of the house. In a typically witty Bridie touch, Mrs McCrimmon ends the play by unconcernedly insisting, despite this amazing occurrence, "Drink up your tea".

Mr Bolfry is set in the Highlands, but it is not a play about the Highlands. Unlike many Scottish dramatists, Bridie did not write over-much about that area of the country, and when he did he largely avoided the bog of romantic cliche into which some of them had fallen. Like *Mr Bolfry* several of his plays have Highland backgrounds — *What it is to be Young*, *The Last Trump*, both of which are set in the contemporary world, and *The Forrigan Reel*, which is a historical fantasy — are in this category. But it is interesting to note how Bridie avoids, as far as he can, depicting the Highlands of the present day as such. Two of the plays just referred to merely use the Highlands as a background and have very few Highland characters in them, while one is historical.

Holy Isle (11 December 1942, Arts Theatre, London) is worthy of some attention. It is a Swiftian fantasy concerning the island of Ultima Thule, the pristine happiness of whose people is threatened by an expedition from Orkney. The first conquerors are civilized by the islanders and a further expedition which arrives decides to withdraw and leave the islanders in peace. There is some pointed satire on colonialism in the first act, and the presentation of the islanders abounds in ironic comment on the shortcomings of civilized humanity. Unfortunately the play tends to fizzle out in the third act and turns sentimental. The characterization is at times inconsistent, but nonetheless it is one of Bridie's better plays, and one in which he exposes with glee the moral limitations of human kind.

The Queen's Comedy (21 August 1950, Glasgow Citizens' Theatre in Lyceum, Edinburgh as part of the Festival) is Bridie's best play. It is set during the Trojan Wars and is concerned with the relationship between men and gods, the effect of the actions of the latter on the lives of the former. Bridie has deliberately used an episodic structure to enable him to present the gods and men alternately throughout the action. Furthermore, in his stage directions he asks for a rostrum on which the scenes in heaven are to be acted, and a fore-stage on which the scenes on earth are to be presented.

The play opens at the bottom of the sea where the gods and goddesses are arguing peevishly with one another over the support being given to Greeks and Trojans by different members of the supernatural fraternity. Bridie has Jupiter reflect on the morality of using men as playthings in heavenly quarrels:

> There are quarter of a million men in the Dardanelles all
> made more or less in my image and capable of rejoicing
> and suffering, of foresight and afterthought. Sometimes up
> there on Mount Ida, when I cannot sleep, I try to put
> myself in their places and wonder what they are thinking.

The play develops the idea that men are made to suffer needlessly as a result of divine whims, and conveys a rather bleak view of the human lot. The ordinary human beings in the play are represented not by the generals who are very closely involved with the gods, but principally by an orderly, an infantryman and Hecamede, a nurse. In their first scene both the orderly and the infantryman take a roughly similar view of the gods, namely that they have a "touch of class" denied the ordinary person, although the orderly considers them a "lazy lot of pushers". As far as the war is concerned, the orderly is in favour of pressing on and defeating the Trojans:

> We've got to show them what we're made of. We canna let
> a lot of Trojan baskets put it across the Greeks. We got an
> ideal to fight for, see.

The infantryman has his doubts, particularly when he looks at the casualties:

Never heard of it. It all come of a bit of square-pushing.
One of them there Trojan Gussies pinched a General's
Judy. What's you and me and that poor write-off over there
got to do with that smooth Cissie and his little bit of
Oojah. We never seen either of them!

On the next occasion when we meet them, the infantryman
shows little sympathy for the orderly's view that the gods are on
the Greek side. The orderly has had a vision of "A popsy about
ninety feet high" (Juno) who had assured him she would see to it
that the Greeks were not defeated. Several scenes later, the
debate about the gods continues between Hecamede and Captain
Machaon. Machaon has a pious attitude towards them which is
not shared by Hecamede. Machaon insists that the gods are
necessary, but Hecamede replies that it would be better to have
human replacements who would at least show sympathy for the
sufferings of ordinary mortals. The present gods are not merely
indifferent to human suffering, they appear to relish it:

— they want to make more birds and stags, flowers and
people to be trapped and trampled and torn. That's really
what they want. That's what it means. What do they care?

The events of the play appear to bear out what Hecamede says.

In the last scene Bridie brings immortals and mortals
together. In Olympus the gods are chatting wittily to each other
and Vulcan is telling unfunny stories, when the shades of those
killed in battle pass through en route to Hades. Mercury catches
a few — Machaon, Hecamede, the orderly and the infantryman
— in a butterfly net. The gods are embarrassed, particularly Juno,
when she is reminded by the orderly of the promise she gave him
in his dreams. The orderly insists on telling the gods what he
thinks of them, before he is returned to the convoy:

Well . . . There you are. You're the push we've been
praying to. "Bless Daddy and Mummy and make Jack a
good boy". Now I seen you I know what's wrong. You sit
up here in your gold settees with a noggin of nectar at your
elbows, tearing on us poor devils like we was terriers and
rats. You great, stupid, lazy, good-looking sticks of barley
sugar! They say you send us the rain and the sunshine and
the wheat in the fields. Well, get on with it and leave us
alone!

It is clear that Bridie's sympathies are with the orderly and Hecamede. The gods have behaved abominably. Their only supporter, Machaon, is an ass. But Bridie does give Jupiter the chance to defend himself:

JUPITER: I soon found that it was easier to make a universe than to control it. It was full of mad, meaningless, fighting forces. I got most of them bound and fixed and working to rules and all of a sudden I felt lonely. I felt that I would rather my mother had given me a puppydog or a kitten. But I should not have made the puppydog or the kitten, so I thought of something else. I found that if I arranged the forces in a certain way, I got a thing called Life. Life is very interesting. I am still working on its permutations and combinations . . . But our poor Shades have long ago missed their convoy. I shall make them into three Stars, I think. I shall call them the Rebels. They will be very interesting to astronomers in a few thousand years.

HECAMEDE: You have not answered us.

JUPITER: Were you asking questions? I am afraid I shall have to refer you to somebody who understands such matters. I don't pretend to understand them myself.

Jupiter's defence is obviously unsatisfactory. He admits he himself does not know the answers. There are, Bridie is implying, no answers to the problem of human suffering, just the reality of suffering itself, in the face of which stoicism is the only defence.

The play can be taken on a metaphysical level. It can also be taken on a more literally down-to-earth level. The gods and the generals can well be compared to the generals in any war, particularly one might suggest, the First World War. Indeed, Bridie's attitude to the generals and gods in *The Queen's Comedy* is remarkably similar to the attitude taken towards the generals in *Oh What a Lovely War!*, namely that they are upper-class amateurs out of touch with, and indifferent to, suffering.

The best evidence for this line of interpretation is to be found in the speech of the orderly already quoted from where he complains about the number of people from whom he has taken orders because he has had to, and to some extent because those who were giving the orders were supposed to know what they were doing. But he has been disillusioned, and has lost all faith in the ideals he believed he was fighting for, not least because of the pretentiousness of the generals, who show the same callousness and indifference as do the gods. The similarities between the gods and the generals is reinforced by Bridie's constant underlining of the fact that they are related to each other. One could argue further that Bridie suggests a clear parallel with the First World War by having Jupiter use the name Dardanelles rather than Hellespont and thus allude to the disastrous campaign of 1915-1916.

The Baikie Charivari (6 October 1952, Citizens') dates from the same period as *The Queen's Comedy* — the end of Bridie's career as a dramatist — and shows a not dissimilar outlook. It is a gloomy pessimistic farewell that Bridie takes of us, reflecting his feelings of disorientation in the post-war world. The play is, however, rather unsatisfactory as drama: the various levels do not cohere properly, the characterization is faulty and there are long, dreich passages which lose the audience's attention.

There can be no question about the great value of Bridie's work for the development of the theatre in Scotland. About his own writing it is difficult to be so certain. Bridie was an extremely prolific writer, and the proliferation of work often leads to a thinness of texture. Plays that suffer from this, although they demonstrate the dramatist's ability to divert an audience with witty dialogue, or interesting turns of plot, lack depth and have little claim on posterity. On the other hand there are a few plays — *The Queen's Comedy* and *Susannah and the Elders* among them — in which Bridie's gifts as an entertainer are combined with an intense concern for his subject matter. There can be little doubt that these plays are of permanent value.

Coming now to Bridie's place in the development of Scottish drama, the first point to be made is that he was the most successful Scottish dramatist commercially that there has yet been. (Barrie apart, and Barrie's base was the English theatre). Although for much of his life he combined writing with medicine, latterly he was able to write full-time and earn a living from it. He could do this because he did not aim at an exclusively Scottish market. He was aiming at the British or English market and many of his plays had their premieres in London. Bridie was an astute man and must have realized early in his career that the way to recognition and financial success was to please the metropolitan audience not the provincial one, though of course it was pleasant to be able to do both.

Of Bridie's full-length stage plays almost two-thirds were premiered south of the border, mostly in London but sometimes elsewhere. *The Anatomist* was his first play to appear in London, in 1930, after the Masque Theatre had presented it in Edinburgh, while *Jonah and the Whale* was his first play to be premiered in the capital, in 1932. Although it lost money, Bridie's plays continued to appear in the city. *A Sleeping Clergyman* after being given its premiere in Malvern ran for two hundred and thirty performances in London. His must successful London presentation was of *Daphne Laureola* in 1949 at Wyndham's Theatre. North of the border four of his plays were premiered by the Scottish National Players and a number by other companies, particularly Glasgow Citizens' towards the end of his career. There have been revivals by Pitlochry Festival Theatre which has presented thirteen of Bridie's plays since 1951.

It might be argued that Bridie sacrificed his Scottishness by aiming so much at the London market. If by this it is meant that he did not write in the Doric, the language of rural lowland Scotland, a case might be made out; but it is doubtful if Bridie was ever interested in the Doric. He aimed to write urbanely and, whatever its merits, the Doric is ill-suited to this purpose. Furthermore, Bridie's artistic concerns, unlike those of some of his contemporaries, were well suited to metropolitan audiences seeking wit, diversion and a dash of philosophy. No writer can escape his background, however, and it has been the argument of this chapter that Bridie's most fundamental attitudes and themes stem directly from his Scottish environment.

This is not to say that Bridie always used Scottish backdrops in his plays. It is one of his merits that his imagination is able to operate against a whole range of backgrounds, Apocryphal, Scottish, English and Trojan. There is, however, a predominance of Scottish backgrounds and the important point here is that it is in the Lowlands of Scotland that Bridie sets many of his plays, not the Highlands. Bridie seems to have been aware of the traps which writing about the Highlands posed, and to have avoided them. Reading and watching his plays set in the Highlands, one is never conscious of a particular background; it could be any one of a number of places.

The same cannot be said of his Lowland backgrounds, for here we are in the world Bridie knew and lived in all his life, the world of the Glasgow middle classes, people wealthy enough to own a substantial residence in the West End and to have a house on the Clyde coast, taken for the season or owned outright. It is a parochial and rather insular world but the combined effects of Glasgow, 'Baikie' and 'Duthie Bay' made such an impression on Bridie that in his work he cannot escape them. Indeed, as has been argued, they represent his fundamental problems as an artist and a man.

At the same time, it must be stressed that although these backgrounds figure much in Bridie's plays, they never render the plays incomprehensible to the outsider. Bridie uses his backgrounds as a series of starting points and the themes that emerge from them are usually generalized. In a sense Bridie could never leave Scotland, but nor did he allow himself to become so bogged down in its minutiae that his work became parochial, as has unfortunately happened with other Scottish writers.

This is part of Bridie's achievement. He has used his environment without becoming submerged in it. On the other hand, it can be argued that his best plays — *Susannah and the Elders* and *The Queen's Comedy* — benefit from not being set against a Scottish backdrop. It is as if in these plays Bridie felt a freedom to explore his ideas that was denied him when he was writing against his native background.

Bridie's achievement rests not only in his gaining recognition on an international scale, but also on his use of the Scottish background and his portrayal of Scottish character. He avoids well the cliches of the stage Scot and gives us a convincing picture of Lowland Scottish people — from the Glasgow bourgeoisie to the 'wee block' like Davie Cooper in *The Golden Legend of Shults*. Despite the excesses of characters like Dr Knox and Charlie Cameron, most of Bridie's Scottish creations are acceptable representations of the Lowland Scot.

This might seem of little account, but it must be remembered that Bridie is the first Scottish dramatist with any claim to international attention. That he attained this attention largely by presenting an accurate contemporary picture of his fellow countrymen on the stage is an achievement that seems remarkable when one considers how little effort was given to the task at the time. As far as Scottish drama is concerned, this is the most encouraging aspect of Bridie's career; the most discouraging aspect is that, despite his achievement, and largely because of his cultural environment, he was not as good as he should have been.

As has been remarked, Bridie's career demonstrated that if the Scottish writer wishes to be successful in financial terms then he must look beyond Scotland to London for his audience. None of the writers we shall be considering later has followed his example — often they have imposed a language barrier themselves — and indeed the only Scot who has in recent years made a success of writing for the London stage is William Douglas-Home. One does not immediately think of him as a Scottish dramatist, rather as a Scot who is making a reasonable income by writing West End plays.

Nor has Bridie's interest in the bourgeoisie been greatly shared by his fellow Scottish dramatists. McLellan as we have seen, has tended to write about the past, as have other less important writers. Only George Reston Malloch in *The Coasts of India* comes near to this aspect of Bridie, although George Munro, whose work will be discussed later, offers a somewhat grimmer picture of Lowland working-class life. Bridie's use of classical and Biblical backgrounds can be paralleled elsewhere in the European theatre; the few plays one has seen in the post-war Scottish theatre which use similar backgrounds may perhaps have been influenced by his work.

We cannot really demonstrate Bridie's influence on a number of other writers. He was and remains an original. That is not to say that his work is in any way a cul-de-sac. Christopher Small argues that Bridie's interest in the Scottish bourgeoisie, indeed his intense dislike of the narrowness and philistinism which he found there, are the most important aspects of his work and ones which do require further development in Scottish dramatic writing. We have yet to see that development.

CHAPTER NINE

The Second World War

THE SECOND WORLD WAR did not have the same effect on the development of the theatre in Scotland as the First. Whereas in 1914 the most promising venture, the Glasgow Repertory Company, came to a sudden end, throughout the Second World War, after the brief period of the closure ordered by the Government in 1939, existing ventures for the most part continued and others were started. This can be attributed to the strength of interest in the theatre which was much more substantial than had been the case in 1914. There were less theatres open in 1939 than there had been in 1914 but it was the music-hall type of theatre that had suffered most from the growth of the cinema; the 'straight' theatres had had much less of a struggle to survive. And of course the great expansion of the amateur movement had ensured that, war or no war, community drama was bound to continue, for all that the one-act festival was suspended during the period of hostilities and other activities had to be curtailed. The growing interest in the theatre which showed itself during the war in support for professional ventures can be attributed in part to the amateur movement. Furthermore, the formation in 1940 of a committee of the Pilgrim Trust — afterwards known as the Council for the Encouragement of Music and the Arts — was indicative of the growing feeling that the performing arts ought to be aided by public bodies.

In Perth when the war came the players continued running the theatre themselves on a non-profit-making basis. The actors did all the work and some of them even slept in the theatre. At the end of a week, after theatrical and living expenses were deducted, the residue, varying between a few shillings and a maximum of three pounds, was divided among them. Despite these privations, in 1941 a Perth Theatre Pageant which included a visit from Bristol Old Vic was sponsored with the help of the CEMA, and a tour of the West and the Highlands organized. Just as the war ended another drama festival opened in Perth, this one under Bridie's patronage.

In 1939 Robert Thornley, an English producer, looked up a gazetteer in order to find the largest town in the United Kingdom which did not have a theatre. And so he brought his company of actors to Dundee, and live drama to a city which the touring companies had by-passed for ten years, leaving it to be content with variety, pantomime and the occasional professional dramatic production. Dundee's first regular theatre had been opened almost a hundred and fifty years previously in 1800, and by 1909 the city had had two substantial playhouses and a number of music halls. However, the onslaught of the cinema was severe in Dundee and by 1930 there was no stage for the legitimate drama.

Financial backing for the minor renaissance of 1939 came from the city itself, in the shape of a £2,000 guarantee fund which was raised principally by the efforts of two local business-men. A non-profit-making company was formed and while negotiations to acquire the Foresters' Hall for transformation into a theatre proceeded, plays were performed in the local amateurs' Little Theatre. Foresters' Hall opened as a theatre in December 1939 with a production of *Hassan*. In the course of the next few years the company required more money, but by 1945 all loans and guarantees had been paid off. Thornley had been succeeded as producer by Anthony Hawtrey, then in 1942 by A. R. Whatmore, who did much to consolidate the position of the Dundee theatre. Whatmore regarded his theatre in many respects as an English repertory which happened to be in Scotland, and consequently showed little interest in Scottish plays: he believed the Scottish public likewise had little interest.

The Byre Theatre in St. Andrews, which as the name implies started life as a cowshed, was let by the Town Council in 1933 to the amateur St. Andrews Play Club, whose members converted the building into a tiny theatre. During the war, for the first time the Byre, which held only seventy-four people and had a stage twelve feet square, was occupied by a small profes-sional company led by Charles Marford who had been stage director at the Old Vic when Lilian Bayliss was running it. Marford tells the story of the Byre during the war in a racily written booklet *The Byre Stormers* which captures very well the spirit of improvization which prevailed. For example, he tells us that in writing a play called *Lade Braes Mystery* he had to so construct it that members of the cast could also be responsible for house management, stage management and lighting.

In the Glasgow area, although the Curtain closed in 1940,

new theatrical ventures continued to appear. One venture, which was shared with Edinburgh, was the Wilson Barrett Company which provided seasons of West End successes and classics throughout the war.

On 2 May 1939 there opened in Rutherglen, in a converted church, a repertory theatre known after its founder Molly S. Urquhart as the MSU Repertory Theatre. The opening production was *The Wind and the Rain* by Merton Hodges. The MSU Rep. survived in this form until 1944 when Molly Urquhart joined the Citizens' Company and the theatre closed temporarily. A few months later, however, a fund was started and the Rutherglen Repertory Company was registered with the aim of founding "a theatre for the development of the drama and dramatic art in Scotland and to encourage a national drama through the production of plays of Scottish life and character". The theatre re-opened and in time was able to engage some full-time professional staff and on occasion to hire professional actors or, more often, pay its part-timers a wage of some sort. During the war years its actors had been amateurs who were given a token payment and included, besides Molly Urquhart herself, Duncan Macrae and Archie Duncan (who both appeared in the second play), Gordon Jackson and Eileen Herlie.

The MSU Theatre did encourage Scottish writers, though paradoxically its 'resident' writer was the Irishman, Paul Vincent Carroll, some of whose work had been performed earlier by the Curtain Theatre, and later was presented by the Citizens.

In 1940 John Stewart, whose father had left him a small fortune amassed by running commercial colleges in Scotland and the north of England, opened the Park Theatre in Woodside Terrace, Glasgow, next door to where the Curtain had been. The theatre, which seated one hundred and six, was extremely well equipped and for seven years of its existence was well supported. Bridie performed the opening ceremony, at which he said: "It may appear daft to start a new little theatre in the middle of the war, but it seems to to have the right kind of lunatic daft Scots panache about it that deserves the very heartiest encouragement, and I believe it is getting that already". He also referred to the number of theatrical ventures there had been in Glasgow, and commented that "anybody who lived in Glasgow must feel a little ashamed, not in the experiments in the theatre that had been made in Glasgow, but at their results".

The Park initially did little for Scottish drama, preferring to concentrate on established successes, but later in its career Scottish plays were performed there, including Bridie's *Jonah 3* and James Shaw Grant's *Tarravore*. Stewart formulated plans for a new theatre in Glasgow after the war which would present specialized dramatic productions and be open to the public, unlike the Park, which was a club. Until such time as this was built, a full-time professional company was to operate in the Park. During the early years of the Park the actors had been amateur, then semi-professional. It was only from 1948 until the theatre closed in 1949 that they were professional. In 1947 property adjoining the existing Park was acquired and plans made for a 500-seater theatre, but building restrictions prevented the plans from becoming a reality. Stewart then turned his attention to realizing his other dream, of a theatre in Pitlochry.

The two most important developments in Glasgow during the war were the Glasgow Citizens' Theatre and Unity Theatre. The Citizens' Theatre was formed with aspirations very similar to previous projects — "with a view to founding the theatre and encouraging a national drama through the production of plays of Scottish life and character". Bridie himself put it in a more practical way:

> *If we are going to have Scottish plays, or plays by Scottish*
> *writers, the Scottish playwright will have to be encouraged.*
> *In Scotland today are many novelists, poets and short story*
> *writers, and we want to see them turning their attention to*
> *the theatre. But unless there is a chance of their plays*
> *having a reasonable run in Scotland, they cannot be*
> *expected to take a real interest in writing for the theatre,*
> *and no one can blame them.* (Scottish Field, *September 1945*)

The story of the founding of the Citizens' Theatre has been told in great detail by Winifred Bannister in her book *James Bridie and His Theatre*. Suffice to say here that Bridie assembled a directorate, consisting of Dr T. J. Honeyman, the then director of Glasgow Art Galleries; Mr George Singleton, owner of the Cosmo Cinema (now the Glasgow Film Theatre); R. W. Greig, Chairman of the Scottish Orchestra; Norman Duthie, an accountant; Paul Vincent Carroll, the dramatist; and Guy McCrone, the novelist. Bridie himself was appointed chairman and, having raised £1,500 in donations, the directors secured a guarantee against loss from the Council for the Encouragement of Music and the Arts. The Athenaeum Theatre, part of the Royal Scottish Academy of Music in Buchanan Street, where it will be recalled the Scottish National Players gave many of their early performances, was chosen as the only suitable and available hall in which to launch the venture, and the name Glasgow Citizens' Theatre, with its allusion to Wareing's earlier company, chosen as a purely temporary measure.

Bridie chose to seek directional talent outside Scotland and approached nineteen different producers before he found one, Jennifer Sounes, willing to come north. On 11 October 1943 the theatre opened with a production of the chairman's own *Holy Isle*. The first season had a shaky start since neither *Holy Isle*, a play which, as has been observed, opens well but fizzles out nor the second production, Goldsmith's *The Good-Natured Man*, were very popular; but with the third presentation, Paul Vincent Carroll's *Shadow and Substance*, the theatre began to establish itself, and when the season ended it was found that the company had broken even.

The second season included three Scottish plays, a revival of John Brandane's *The Treasure Ship* and premieres of Joe Corrie's *A Master of Men* and Bridie's *The Forrigan Reel*. The inclusion of these plays in the programme and of a number of actors in the company who had previously worked with one of the smaller amateur or semi-professional groups, for example Duncan Macrae and Molly Urquhart (both formerly with the Curtain and MSU Theatres), James Gibson (Scottish National Players) and Gordon Jackson (MSU) indicates clearly the debt the Citizens' owed to the ventures of the inter-war period which had encouraged and developed both Scottish writing and Scottish acting.

When the second season ended, the necessity to call up the CEMA guarantee had still not arisen. During the season two tours had been undertaken, one of the continent with *The Forrigan Reel* and one of the West of Scotland with *Mr Bolfry*. On the Scottish tour there had been good houses, although support was much better in small towns than in the large industrial ones. Members of the company commented favourably on the effect which the amateur movement seemed to have had in building up an interest in drama.

As the popularity of the Citizens' Theatre grew, it was

realized that a better theatre was required. By an extremely fortunate coincidence Harry McKelvie, the owner of the 1,000-seater Royal Princess's Theatre, situated near Gorbals Cross, was finding that his health was no longer up to the ardours of running the pantomime seasons for which the theatre was famous. He offered the building on a ten-year lease to the Citizens' company at an annual rent of £1,000 over that period (he paid the first year's amount himself) provided that the total sum was guaranteed. A gift from a leading industrialist, Sir Frederick Stewart, of £10,000 met these conditions and on 31 March 1945 the last performance was given in the Athenaeum. The Citizens' opened in the Gorbals the following autumn.

The theatre to which they transferred had been opened in 1878 as Her Majesty's by James McFadyen. After an unsuccessful six months with a varied programme it closed, but was re-opened in 1879 by Harcourt Beryl as the Royal Princess's. A programme of melodrama, variety and pantomime proved successful and was continued under Beryl's former assistant, Richard Waldon. As Victorian melodrama died pantomime became more important, and Harry McKelvie, who took over after Waldon's death in 1922, set out to make the Royal Princess's the home of pantomime. Each show ran from December till the summer when the theatre closed until the following year's pantomime opened, usually preceded by a variety show. For years McKelvie and George West, sticking to a very rigid dramatic pattern, worked together on the pantomime in which West also starred. Obviously the theatre has now changed its nature, but the Citizens' company have for most of the period of their existence endeavoured with varying success to mount a Christmas show which owes something to the theatre's pantomime tradition.

In complete contrast to what might be regarded as the 'bourgeois' Citizens', there was established, initially on an amateur basis, a proletarian committed theatre in Glasgow. Unity Theatre came into being in 1941, under the impetus of the Unity Theatre movement elsewhere in Britain and was formed by amateurs from various Glasgow clubs, the Workers' Theatre Group, the Clarion Players, the Transport Players and the Jewish Institute Players. The members of this group sought a more socially involved theatre than existed at the time, and aimed to draw in working-class audiences. They included some

Communists and Marxists, but it would be wrong to assume that Unity was a highly doctrinaire body more interested in politics than theatre. This was not the case, although there was a strong sense of social commitment. A dozen productions were mounted during war time but it was in the post-war period that Unity made its bid for permanence.

At the end of the war, in an attempt to put their venture on a firmer footing and possibly mindful of the failure of the Scottish National Players when they did not grasp a similar opportunity, Unity decided to form a professional company of players as London Unity had done. Thereafter there were two Unity companies, one amateur, whose productions were mainly directed by Donald McBean formerly of the Transport Players, and one professional under the directorship of Robert Mitchell of the Glasgow Players. The professional company, which made its debut on 9 April 1946 in O'Casey's *Purple Dust*, had ten members in addition to the director and stage-staff, and this meant a considerable income was necessary to sustain operations. Although Unity had played in the Athenaeum Theatre during the war, since its availability was restricted after 1945, the professional company played whenever it could and in addition toured throughout Scotland, playing regularly in Edinburgh and other centres. Several visits were made to London towards the end of Unity's career. The part-time company's activities were more intermittent, but it too was peripatetic.

As one would have expected, the main problem was finance. When the professional company was formed, Unity had only a few hundred pounds in the bank, a comfortable position for an amateur club, but hardly a very firm basis for a venture of this kind being undertaken. Throughout the professional company's existence the amateur company, or part-time company as it was known, continued to provide a subsidy. Other revenue came from the box office, principally from Robert McLeish's *The Gorbals Story* which was Unity's best money-spinner, and for a time from the Arts Council, but this support was withdrawn as a consequence of what Bridie, who would appear to have had a hand in the withdrawal, called its "scatterbrained finance". So far as can be judged thirty years later, this charge had some substance in it. Unity did not apparently show much business acumen, though for a time under the supervision of Oscar Loewenstein, who was employed for a year as business manager, a saner approach to financial matters was employed. But neither Mr Loewenstein, nor the income from amateur activities, nor the royalties from a film of *The Gorbals Story* was enough to save the venture. Unity petered out rather than stopped at the end of the forties and some of its debts have never been cleared. The amateur side continued for a time but it too petered out in the fifties.

Despite its sad demise Unity did made an important contribution. In the first place it helped keep theatre going during the war and extended the range of drama available to the Glaswegian and Scottish public after the war. It could claim to have founded the Edinburgh Festival Fringe since it performed McLellan's *Torwatletie* and a Scots version of *The Lower Depths* without official support at the first festival in 1947. Most importantly it introduced a new dimension to Scottish theatre.

One of the criticisms that has been made of the Scottish National Players in this study is that much of the drama they presented bore little relationship to the lives of the ordinary population of the country, in particular the lives of the urban population. Unity deliberately sought to make up for this failure. The evidence lies in the programmes of work presented, in which Clifford Odets, Sean O'Casey and Maxim Gorki feature prominently; the work of these writers was usually related in production to a Scottish context. Unity also sponsored a visit to Glasgow by the then young Theatre Workshop in 1946. In addition Unity presented a fair number of new plays by Scottish authors with social themes. *The Gorbals Story*, which is concerned with the housing problem, is the most obvious example, but there are others. James Barke's *Major Operation* presents the world of the Clyde shipyard worker and his place in the class struggle, a theme returned to more recently in Bill Bryden's *Willie Rough*. The same author contributed *The Night of the Big Blitz* and *When the Boys Come Home*, also set in Clydebank. George Munro's *Gold in his Boots* is concerned with the sordid underworld of professional football. Benedict Scott in *The Lambs of God* tackled the subject of homosexuality against the background of the Depression, while Ena Lamont Stewart in *Starched Aprons* examined the exploitation of the nursing profession.

As evidence of the ideological motivation behind Unity there is the magazine *Scots Theatre* published by the group for a short period in 1946 and 1947. Each copy of the magazine bore on the front cover a quotation from Gorki: "The theatre is the school of the people — it makes them think and it makes them feel . . .". An editorial declared:

> *Today we have Unity Theatre established as the most vital native cultural influence in Scotland. Its actors, playwrights and technicians have been drawn from the ranks of ordinary working people, whose background and everyday life is identical with the masses who form its audiences.*

That many people in Unity were convinced that they were moving the Scottish theatre in a new direction is clear:

> *In the new Scottish theatre there are two divisions: primarily middle-class repertories and writers whose art is seen in Perth, the Glasgow Citizens' Theatre and elsewhere: and the tougher working-class drama and performances to be seen at Glasgow Unity Theatre.*

For Unity, theatre meant commitment. Robert Mitchell declared that "one of Unity's main conceptions was that of the theatre marching in line with social policy". One notes in reviews of productions by other companies in *Scots Theatre* a certain intolerance of plays which lack social commitment. A review of a production of *In Good King Charles' Golden Days*, for example, sneered at the "elite" who people this play.

It is interesting to note that Unity too, like so many Scottish theatrical enterprises, looked to the Irish example but from a left-wing viewpoint:

> *. . . we pray for the time when a Scotsman will emulate the great Irishman (O'Casey) and produce such plays of the people.*

The political orientation can be viewed with mixed feelings. On the positive side, Unity attempted to make the theatre meaningful to ordinary people and seems to have succeeded for a time in doing so. Working people came, though not in the numbers that Unity would have liked, and watched plays which they could relate to their own lives. On the negative side, the left-wing commitment of Unity would in the long term have proved a limitation, for to judge by some of the writing in *Scots*

Theatre it might well have blinded its members to the merits of dramatic writing without obvious political content. However this is perhaps to carp, and it must be emphasized that it is quite wrong to think that all Unity members were committed socialists or adhered to the opinions and views expressed in *Scots Theatre*; many were simply interested in the theatre.

Several of Unity's actors joined the ranks of the professionals, among them Archie Duncan, Russell Hunter, Andrew Keir, Roddy McMillan and Marjorie Thomson, and one can still see a proletarian vitality in the work of these artists today. It was said of Unity that its techniques were those of Stanislawski, but in practice they were based on those of the British stage at the time, with an infusion of a strong feeling for contemporary urban Scotland. Reviews of their productions often use such terms as 'sincerity' and 'conviction' — sometimes, it must be said, in rather a patronising fashion.

It would be foolish to pretend that Unity's contribution was a great one, but it could have been. Lack of money, financial mismanagement, the absence of a permanent home, all prevented it from realizing its full potential. Its achievement remains the progress it did make towards its self-declared objectives of presenting socially aware plays and bringing working-class people into the theatre. That it was unable to realize these aims completely is a loss the Scottish theatre has yet to make up, although the 7:84 Theatre Company (Scotland) is currently pursuing similar objectives. It could of course be said that it was naive of Unity to expect that it could break down the social and educational barriers that divide the mass of our population from the arts and that its approach had more in common with the battering ram than with the sophisticated methods of persuasion open to those who would seek to win the support of the masses. But before people can begin to appreciate the subtleties and complexities of art they must be excited by it. Unity for a time provided that excitement.

CHAPTER TEN
The Theatre in Scotland since the War

WE HAVE A SITUATION TODAY that is in many ways the reverse of
the one we started with at the beginning of the century. It will be
recalled that then the commercial theatre, the music hall and
the pantomime were all flourishing. Only the repertory theatre
movement was struggling for audiences and finance. As cinema
wiped out the music hall and put pressure on the commercial
theatre, the audience narrowed — the working class in abandon-
ing the music hall for the cinema cut itself off from live theatre,
and now it draws its dramatic sustenance from television —
cinema in its turn having been partially abandoned. In this
situation only a theatre which drew on the support of a committed
audience could survive and only then with large subventions
from public funds. The post-war theatrical audience is largely a
middle-class professional one, more dedicated to theatre as a
serious art form than the audiences at the beginning of the
century but it is an interesting paradox that this elite group of
theatre-goers depends for its pleasures on subsidies through
taxation from the numerically far larger social groups which
ignore the theatre in favour of other pursuits.

Occasionally one sees in the press expressions of resentment
at this situation, usually when a particular theatrical production
has been controversial enough to move on to the news pages.
Theatregoers tend to laugh or sneer at uninformed attacks on
'sex and filth' and at the protests about public money being
wasted on such socially useless extravagances. It is a mistake to
sneer, for such protest — however misguided it may seem —
highlights the iniquities of a situation when the many are paying
to subsidize the pleasures of the few, a few who are probably
better able to pay in full for their enjoyment than many other
social groups. We all know that a civilized society should be able
to provide decent housing for its citizens and cultural recreation
for them, but so long as we fail to provide the former, attacks
are going to be made. And they will continue until such time as
theatre develops into less of a minority art form and attracts its
audiences from a far wider social spectrum than it does at the
moment. Efforts have been made in this direction: we can cite

the various Theatre in Education projects, the growth in local arts centres, the tours of the 7:84 Company which attempt to take theatre out to the people. There is however a great deal of progress still required and, to be honest, much of the blame for the lack of such progress must rest squarely with the theatres themselves: as long as they give the impression by their general atmosphere that there is something superior about the theatre, then ordinary people will continue to be put off and will stay away. It ought also to be said that as long as our education system continues to throw over half of the nation's children out of school at sixteen, having given them little or no chance to develop their appreciation of the arts, and to treat those who remain only slightly better, then it is futile to expect vast audiences for theatre, opera or orchestral concerts.

These remarks may not seem original. They are not meant to be. It is important to re-assert facts that are obvious until such time as action is taken. Social justice is not the only consideration involved; there is the simple selfish point that the arts — for all the huge increase in public support that we have seen in recent years — are vulnerable in times of public expenditure cutbacks and will remain vulnerable until such time as the majority of people are no more prepared to do without theatres and concert halls than hospitals and housing.

The post-war period to which we now turn has been one of growth and decline in the Scottish theatre as it has been in the British theatre as a whole, and although it would be idle to pretend that we now have an exceptionally vigorous and flourishing theatre, equally it would be wrong to deny the steady progress that has been made. Progress has, in the main, been in the field of repertory theatre and this has taken place against the background of the development of television, the growth of which can be gauged from the following figures:

BROADCASTING RECEIVING LICENCES IN SCOTLAND

	Radio Licences	TV Licences	Combined Licences	Colour Licences
1952	1,139,927	41,699		
1962	308,584	1,119,824		
1972	—	—	1,517,795	182,594

Whereas previously radio's audience did not appear to be growing at the expense of the cinema, but alongside it, television soon began to eat into the cinema audience, as the figures given below indicate.

CINEMAS IN SCOTLAND

	Total	Aberdeen	Dundee	Edinburgh	Glasgow
1950	617	17	25	33	106
1960	476	15	22	26	69
1970	254	12	10	16	36

Admissions dropped at a corresponding rate (*figures in 000's*):

1950:	186,500
1960:	66,769
1970:	22,634

Theatre has, of course, suffered alongside the cinema:

THEATRES IN SCOTLAND

	Total	Aberdeen	Dundee	Edinburgh	Glasgow
1950	29	3	1	5	10
1960	22	3	1	5	7
1970	15	1	1	3	4

The theatres that have been most subject to closure are the larger theatres offering variety shows, such as the Edinburgh and Glasgow Empires, which closed in 1962 and 1963 respectively. The theatres that have survived and grown are those with which television is in less direct competition, the repertory theatres. But they have only kept alive because of subsidies from public funds which did not previously exist.

It is pertinent to note that when the unsubsidized Wilson Barrett Company ceased operations in 1955 television was named as the cause of its demise. The company had been formed in 1938 shortly after the Brandon-Thomas company, of which Barrett had been a member, was disbanded. Initially it played in London and the provinces including Scotland, but when its metropolitan base was blitzed in 1941 it came north permanently, and thereafter played in Edinburgh and Glasgow and to a lesser extent in Aberdeen. A short-lived attempt to fill the gap left by the disbanding of the Wilson Barrett company was made by Henry Sherek in conjunction with Howard and Wyndham, but the Henry Sherek Players ceased their presentations after one season in 1956, during which two companies performed in Edinburgh and Glasgow under the leadership of

Duncan Macrae and Stanley Baxter, and a number of Scottish writers, including Robert Kemp and Alexander Reid, had work performed.

We find then that each Scottish city has closed some theatres. This problem has been slightly alleviated by the King's Theatres in Edinburgh and Glasgow and Her Majesty's in Aberdeen passing into the hands of the local authorities, but so far it has proved difficult to reconcile the need to provide a stage for the infrequent visits of the national companies and the need to operate these theatres throughout the year without running up too large a deficit.

Property developers have not been slow to realize the advantages of the excellent sites occupied by many theatres and, in a declining theatrical situation, the pressure for 'redevelopment' has been another factor leading to closure by owners who did not consider that they were receiving an adequate return on their capital any more. The Glasgow Pavilion is the only major theatre still in private hands that has not been redeveloped.

Touring, often the mainstay of the larger theatres in the provinces, has also been declining, particularly since the triumph of television. The closure of the Empire in Glasgow in 1963 could be regarded as symbolizing the end of variety and light entertainment tours, although the tradition is not yet totally extinct. While plays continue to be toured, with the support of either commercial managements or the Arts Council, it is an operation which has been on the decline, although there are a few signs at the moment of writing that the situation may be changing.

Recently, very few tours from London have reached Scotland. As will be recalled, one of the stock criticisms of the Scottish theatrical situation in the past was its over-dependence on London tours. This criticism no longer applies and there is no doubt that, while it is unfortunate that the national companies in particular do not tour very much, it is a distinct improvement that so much internal Scottish theatrical activity is being generated, as is now the case.

One highly acceptable consequence of the growth of television that should be emphasized by way of balance has been the expansion of employment opportunities for Scottish actors and writers. This has the advantage that by providing lucrative employment it enables artists to undertake work in the theatre that otherwise would be financially ruinous to them. It thus acts as a patron of live drama.

We come now to a consideration of the repertory theatre situation and the first thing to be noted is that several of the ventures which started in 1945 have continued their work. For example, in 1946 Perth Rep. became a non-profit-making organization which obtained financial assistance from the Arts Council. It was managed by Marjorie Dence from 1947 till her death in 1966 and in 1968 the theatre was bought by Perth Town Council and is now a civic theatre.

The Dundee Rep., which was established in 1939, has continued to exist despite the major set-back it received in 1963 when the theatre in Nicoll Street was destroyed by fire. Since that time the company has played in a converted church which is not well situated from a business point of view and as a result has lost part of its audience. It was hoped that a new theatre complex would be built on a site provided by the University of Dundee and that the Repertory Company would be given a home in this complex. At the time of writing however the situation is extremely uncertain, the existing building having come to the end of its useful life and no obvious replacement being available.

After the war the Byre at St. Andrews was taken over by the Play Club who finished the job of converting the old cowshed. From that time the theatre and its successor, the new Byre (opened in 1970) has been occupied from April to December by a small professional company who are responsible for all the work involved — acting, production, making scenery and publicity. The business side of the organization is attended to by the Byre Theatre of St. Andrews Ltd. (formerly the Play Club). One of the advantages of this system is that young actors and technicians have an opportunity to stretch themselves much sooner than would be possible in a larger repertory company.

The MSU Repertory Theatre had closed down in 1944 when Molly Urquhart joined the Citizens' Theatre Company, but in 1945 it re-opened as a result of local fund-raising as the Rutherglen Repertory Theatre. It operated with amateur and semi-professional actors and some permanent professional staff until 1959, when it finally closed.

Of the new theatres since the war the Pitlochry Festival Theatre has perhaps the most unexpected setting. It was the creation of John Stewart, who established the Park Theatre in Glasgow. He aimed to provide a Scottish Malvern and to this end he acquired Knockendarroch House in Pitlochry and drew up plans for erecting a theatre in the grounds. However, he could not obtain building permission because of post-war restrictions, so on 19 May 1951 the theatre opened in a tent which held five hundred people, in front of a wide stage. In 1953 a semi-permanent building was put up. It seats five hundred and two in an open fan-shaped auditorium, again in front of a wide stage, forty-four feet across. John Stewart remained director until his early death in 1957, and then Kenneth Ireland, formerly Stewart's general manager at both the Park and Pitlochry, took over. Pitlochry has been a successful theatre, doubling its attendance figures since 1951 and playing consistently in recent years to almost seventy per cent of capacity. Nonetheless, it too has had its share of financial problems, and was only rescued from a crisis recently by the generous response to a public appeal. Plans for a permanent building have been prepared and ground acquired.

Edinburgh, for so long without a permanent professional repertory company, has increased its theatrical amenities considerably since the war. For the previous twenty years efforts had been made to establish such a company, but to little avail. At the end of the war, however, there were some professional performances in the Little Theatre, Pleasance under the auspices of 'Everyman Theatre'. A short season was mounted from October 1945 to January 1946 by a company of which Duncan Macrae was a member.

In 1944 the Home Board of the Church of Scotland had received the anonymous donation of a block of property in Elm Row, Edinburgh, which included a theatre then in use as a cinema. The theatre was re-opened as the Gateway in 1946 under the management of the Church. For the next few years plays (amateur and professional) and films were presented, some though by no means all of which had broadly religious themes. As a result of the difficulties involved, stemming mainly from lack of expertise and the absence of the continuity which only a permanent professional group would give, it was decided in 1953 to lease the theatre to an independent company which would be responsible for the presentation of plays and the running of the theatre.

In this way the Gateway Company was formed under the chairmanship of Robert Kemp, the Church advising on but not dictating programme policy. The company opened in October 1953 with a production of *The Forrigan Reel*, and from then until 1965 provided regular repertory programmes in Edinburgh. The company had problems, not unlike those of the other theatres which have been discussed, principally lack of money and the difficulty of holding an audience for a widely varying programme. The worst crisis seems to have been in 1960 when the theatre came close to shutting down. A crisis of a different kind arose when the company decided to put on Aristophanes' *Lysistrata* and a board member resigned. The play was not presented. However, the most important achievement of the Gateway Company was that it maintained professional repertory theatre in Edinburgh for twelve seasons until the Edinburgh Civic Theatre was set up. The success of the Civic Theatre at the present moment must be due in some degree to the audience-building done by the Gateway.

The Edinburgh Civic Theatre Trust was established in 1965 and Tom Fleming was appointed director of the venture which was to operate in the Royal Lyceum Theatre. The Gateway Company, having considered the possibility of existing alongside the Civic Theatre, decided that this was not a viable proposition. Since 1965, therefore, repertory has been provided in Edinburgh by the Civic Theatre. The first season was adventurous, but did not attract large audiences to several of its productions. Subsequently Mr Fleming was replaced by Clive Perry, an Englishman who is largely responsible for building up the company's audiences and reputation to their present high levels. Mr Perry became Edinburgh's director of theatres, a post from which he resigned in 1976. His successor as director of the Lyceum Company, Stephen Macdonald, was previously artistic director at Dundee, and a decade before that an actor of considerable distinction at the Citizens' Theatre in Glasgow.

The Lyceum's principal problem is the old building in which it operates: if the proposed Opera House complex had been constructed it was expected that some kind of provision would be made for the company, but the project has been abandoned after years of delay. It is now the intention that the company should stay in the Lyceum building and the studio theatre (opened in nearby premises in 1975) and that substantial renovations be undertaken. Work on front of house facilities was completed in 1977, but enlargement of premises backstage is still needed.

In Glasgow since the end of the war the story of the Citizens' has been one of varied fortune. Audience figures have continually fluctuated. The advent of television had the same effect that it had all over the country when attendance figures at theatres showed a sharp drop. During the early sixties the audiences began to build up again but towards the end of the decade dropped to frightening levels (in one year the company was playing to something like thirty per cent of capacity). Many reasons were advanced for the decline, which has since been corrected to some extent and this was not echoed at the time in other Scottish reps. It was suggested that the theatre's position in an unattractive part of the city had been made worse by the slum clearance round about. The building itself has been under sentence of death for some years and present progress towards building a replacement is slow.

There are, however, other more fundamental reasons. When the Citizens' began, its links with Glasgow were strong. Local actors and actresses like Molly Urquhart and Duncan Macrae were known and liked by the audiences. Other local talent in the shape of, for example, Stanley Baxter and John Cairney could be seen developing on the Citizens' stage. A genuinely Scottish — not to say Glaswegian — company of actors who could play in not only Scots comedy but in all kinds of drama, was being established. Over the years this has come to be less the case. Likewise the company's artistic directors have more and more been Englishmen who, no matter how dedicated, are bound to regard the Citizens' as a stepping stone to other jobs, usually in the south. Michael Blakemore, for example, was associate director at the Citizens' in the mid-sixties before moving to the National Theatre. In fairness to the present incumbent, Giles Havergal, it ought to be stressed that he has held the post since 1969. Nonetheless the link between the Citizens' and its traditional audiences, which was provided by a predominantly Scottish company, has disappeared to the theatre's detriment, although the company has sought in the last few years to build a relationship with a new younger audience.

If one major development since the war has been the growth in the number of repertory theatres, the other has been the establishment of two club theatres, the Traverse and the Close.

"The Traverse has always been, and will continue to be, about what is new" — this declaration made by the theatre itself sums up the nature of the Traverse. It has consistently presented new and experimental work, often of a highly controversial nature. The Traverse was established in 1963 under the chairmanship and later directorship of Jim Haynes, a young American living and working in Edinburgh, in premises near St. Giles Cathedral, formerly a lodging house of dubious repute called Kelly's Paradise. The room used as the auditorium held sixty spectators on either side of an acting area. In 1969 the Traverse moved to new premises in the Grassmarket where, in addition to better administrative and social facilities, the theatre has a multi-purpose acting area in which audiences ranging in size from twelve to a hundred and twenty can be seated. Plans for an expansion of the existing premises to incorporate two auditoria have reached an advanced stage.

There can be little doubt that the Traverse has not merely made Edinburgh more interesting theatrically and livened up the Festival with three weeks of frenetic artistic activity, but also made Scotland more aware of what is happening elsewhere. The Traverse has not only been a haven for experiment, but also a weapon against cultural insularity. An attempt to establish a second Traverse company in 1970, the Traverse Workshop Company, was not however successful. A venture, somewhat akin to the Traverse in spirit, the Pool Lunchtime Theatre, opened in Edinburgh in 1971 but petered out three years later after presenting a varied and interesting series of programmes.

The Close Theatre Club (which in 1973 was unfortunately, like so many previous Glasgow theatres, destroyed by fire) opened in 1965 'up a close' next to the Citizens' in Glasgow as part of the older organization, sharing actors and other facilities. The small acting area was surrounded by banked rows of seats on three sides and thus an intimacy between actors and audience, not possible in the Citizens' itself, could be achieved.

Mention ought also to be made, when surveying the contemporary theatrical scene, of the Mull Little Theatre established in Dervaig on Mull by Barrie and Marianne Hesketh in 1967, initially as an adjunct to their very agreeable boarding house, and then as a full-time enterprise in its own right. This extremely small company now presents especially scaled-down productions of large-cast plays, as well as small-cast ones, in Mull itself and throughout Scotland, and represents an experiment of a different kind from that found at the Traverse and the Close.

Another venture owing much to private initiative is the Ochtertyre Theatre opened by Sir William Murray at his home near Crieff in 1971. Despite the wide range of dramatic and musical performances presented, the theatre has looked in vain for significant support from public funds and was only saved from closure in 1976 when a new-found patron of some distinction, Bing Crosby, came to its aid.

Finally we must mention the activities of the 7:84 Theatre Company, a Scottish offshoot of the English company of the same name — a name which alludes to the alleged fact that seven per cent of the population of Britain own 84 per cent of the country's wealth. This embryonic agit-prop company has toured Scotland with a number of exhilarating and polished productions which display a very obvious and perhaps naive left-wing commitment, as did for example their first and greatest success in 1973 *The Cheviot, the Stag and the Black Black Oil* which sought to relate the Highland Clearances with the current rush for oil. Whether 7:84 marks the beginning of popular Scottish political theatre — taking drama to the people in halls, community centres and clubs — remains to be seen. Interestingly it recalls two ventures discussed earlier, the Scottish National Players who toured with comparable enthusiasm, and Unity who had a similar social commitment. 7:84 is different from these two: for one thing it is fully professional and for another much of its material is produced by the combination of a rough script usually written by John McGrath with actors' improvisation, often of the most hilarious kind. Yet again its social commitment is overtly Marxist — much more so than Unity's — and the company is beginning to run the risk of productions that do not cohere: the satirical sketches remain amusing and inventive, the political diatribes become boring and repetitive.

Turning now from the growth of theatre buildings and companies to a consideration of the programmes of plays presented, we find that the most consistent attempt in recent years to present the plays of living Scottish writers alongside a varied international repertoire, which is clearly the best combination, was at the Gateway: included among the authors it supported were Robert McLellan, Robert Kemp, Alexander Reid, A. B. Paterson, T. M. Watson, Ada F. Kay, Moray McLaren and James Scotland. The Gateway felt itself somewhat alone in its commitment to the Scottish dramatist. As Moultrie Kelsall, chairman of the Company from 1960-65, has commented:

> *The fact is that comparatively few of the Scottish plays first produced by the Edinburgh Gateway Company had subsequent professional productions (though some were performed by amateurs) and until there is a better market for them they're likely to remain few and far between. We did our best to create such a market, but with insufficient support from other theatres in Scotland. Possibly they weren't always impressed by the plays: possibly they doubted whether they had an audience for them; but the basic reason, I believe, is that they haven't shared to the same extent our missionary zeal for providing a stage on which native drama could grow.*

That the Gateway company was aware that it was only through practice that Scottish writers could learn their craft, and that it is the Scottish theatre's responsibility to provide the opportunity for that practice, is in itself a tribute. It is, of course, no coincidence that Mr Kelsall was previously associated with the Scottish National Players.

The company encouraged Scottish actors. There was an attempt to build up a Scottish company, capable of presenting Scottish plays. Actors of the stature of Tom Fleming, Lennox Milne, Roddy MacMillan and Duncan Macrae worked for the Gateway. Many young actors began their careers there. The Lyceum company initially did not continue the Gateway's policy but recently has shown marked signs of moving in its direction, particularly while Bill Bryden was an associate director from 1971-1975, when new Scottish work by Stewart Conn, Roddy MacMillan and Bryden himself was presented. Indeed the Lyceum Company has now such a high proportion of Scottish actors that it was able to boast that its 1975 revival of *The Flouers o Edinburgh* was the first production of the play to have all the Scottish parts played by Scottish actors.

The most noteworthy event in the history of Perth Theatre in recent years was the attempt by Iain Cuthbertson, who was director during the 1967-68 season, to mount a programme which contained a very large proportion of Scottish plays and Scottish documentary-type plays. Unfortunately the financial return was not sufficient to justify further expenditure, and so Cuthbertson recommended termination of the venture. Since that time a much more conservative policy has been pursued, with the main emphasis on comedy. It would be easy to adduce this setback as evidence that Scottish theatre does not work. A more sensible conclusion would be that to go from one extreme (a modest company not taking too many risks) to another (a company twenty-seven-strong and a very ambitious programme) is foolhardy.

At Dundee the company's policy did not change drastically in the post-war period, although there were more attempts to present material with a local flavour than was the case previously. The policy has now taken a decidedly new direction, and greater emphasis is being put on presenting Scottish plays.

Since 1951 at Pitlochry there have been annual seasons, during which an average of six plays has been presented. Inevitably, since it operates in a tourist centre during the summer, and consequently depends largely on the holiday trade, the theatre has had to maintain a broad appeal. Therefore the lighter kind of play has tended to predominate, though the theatre has also mounted productions of plays by Ibsen, Pirandello, Chekhov, Tourneur, Webster and Shakespeare. Scottish drama has been represented by revivals of plays mainly by Bridie and Barrie, and occasional premieres. New writing until recently has been inadequately represented in Pitlochry's programmes, but now modern Scottish drama in particular seems to have found a permanent place in the repertoire. Tom Gallacher has been particularly well supported by the Highland theatre.

If we examine the programmes of Glasgow Citizens' Theatre over the years, we must note the proportionately smaller place occupied by Scottish plays, particularly new Scottish plays, in recent times. The first season at the Royal Princess's was almost entirely occupied by Scottish pieces, over half of them premieres. While the proportion of Scottish plays decreased (quite rightly) during the next few seasons, there were still premieres of several new pieces each year. Until the end of the fifties authors such as James Bridie, Robert McLellan, Robert Kemp, Robins Millar, Eric Linklater, Alexander Reid, Alexander Scott, George Munro and James Scotland had plays performed at the Citizens'. In the sixties the pattern began to change. Fewer and fewer Scottish plays were presented, and even fewer premieres, until by the end of the decade virtually no Scots plays, new or old, were being presented.

Under the artistic direction of Giles Havergal the Citizens' has tended to interest itself in spectacular presentation and to see itself as being in the van of international theatrical development. While this is a perfectly legitimate view for the company to take of its work, it has not been to the advantage of Scottish plays. Successive directors before Mr Havergal did insist that they were only too willing to present Scottish plays if good ones appeared. What they seemed to forget is that good new plays do not suddenly appear, but are preceded by mediocre work. One of the principal reasons for the emergence of the Scottish writers whose plays were presented at the Citizens' during the first half of its life was the existence of the amateur drama movement between the wars. This movement, despite its deficiencies, was often willing to present plays of little worth, and it thus enabled writers to benefit from seeing their own work and the work of other people performed. So they were able to learn from their mistakes and develop. No such opportunity exists on any scale today, despite the brave but intermittent efforts of odd amateur clubs here and there. It is thus unrealistic for theatre directors to expect fully-fledged writers to appear and knock on their doors. Only apprentices will present themselves, and if they are never given the opportunity to learn their trade they will remain apprentices. This fact has been hesitantly recognized by some Scottish theatres in the mounting of occasional drama workshops where excerpts from new plays are performed and discussed: Pitlochry has made such workshops a permanent feature of its programmes. The Scottish Society of Playwrights, a body formed in 1974 to promote the work of Scottish dramatists, has also organized such workshops.

As far as the Citizens' is concerned, interest in fostering Scottish drama has so far declined that Tony Paterson, the literary adviser appointed specifically to encourage native talent in the late sixties, resigned since there had ceased to be any chance of the work he was nurturing ever being presented. It remains a matter for regret then that the Citizens' management does not feel able to find a place for Scottish plays in its repertoire except when performed by visiting companies.

The Traverse, being a private club, was able to operate without recourse to the Lord Chamberlain before the abolition of theatre censorship and this meant that the choice of play was wider than what was available to the reps. Well over one hundred world and British premieres have been presented, including work by Arrabal, Billetdoux, Gunter Grass, Mrozek, Lawrence and Olwen Wymark. The theatre has seen itself for most of its life as a show case for the best of international experimental drama, but it has not neglected Scottish authors. In particular it has nurtured two writers, one an expatriate Scot, Cecil Taylor, and the other an expatriate Englishman working in Scotland, Stanley Eveling. Several plays by both Taylor and Eveling have been premiered at the Traverse and have later gone on to London. The Traverse has tried to 'relate' to the Scottish environment. As Jim Haynes has put it:

> I'm very interested in the theatre having local relevance and when I was in Scotland I think I put on more plays by Scottish writers than possibly any other theatre producer, not because they were Scottish but because their plays had local relevance. I really think the theatre should reflect its environment. (Scottish Theatre, June 1969)

One might dispute Mr Haynes' personal claims, but not that the attempt to relate was made. Under Chris Parr's directorships — he was appointed in 1975 — the Traverse has sought to present a programme balance between English and Scottish plays with less emphasis on the European and world theatre. Scottish writers who have benefited from this policy include Donald Campbell, Tom McGrath and Hector MacMillan.

Initially it was thought that the Close would be a Glasgow equivalent of Edinburgh's Traverse, but that was not to be. Although great use was made of the intimacy afforded by the Close, and plays by such writers as Beckett, Albee and Strindberg were given productions which would not otherwise have been seen in Glasgow, genuine experimentation was limited. Indeed, possibly the most experimental and exhilarating production, *Dr Faustus* directed by Charles Marowitz, resulted within a few months of the Close opening in a public uproar initiated by the management committee of the theatre itself. This revolved round the question of whether the production was insulting to the Queen or not and, like so many of Glasgow's artistic controversies, served only to divert attention from what was actually being attempted theatrically. We need not condemn the Close's committee. It is a reasonable assumption that they were reflecting the views of the membership. What we can conclude is that the Glasgow theatrical public was not at that time so receptive to genuine experiment as the Edinburgh one and, if the Close were to stay in business, the people who ran it always had to bear this in mind. Times change, of course, and audiences twelve years later can blink in astonishment at what happens on the stage of The Citizens.

The Byre for its part has premiered a number of Scottish plays, including several by its founder, A. B. Paterson.

The Edinburgh Festival's contribution to Scottish theatre has been disappointing. The emphasis in the Festival has always been musical and its achievements in that sphere remain substantial. The plastic arts on the other hand have played an increasingly subsidiary role. There have always been a fairly respectable number of plays performed each year. Criticism has tended to be directed at the quality of drama rather than the quantity. Such criticism should not, however, blind us to the value of seeing a variety of companies from overseas and to the worth of some of the productions mounted in recent years by, for example, the Prospect Theatre and the Actors Company, which made its debut at the 1972 Festival.

Among the Festival's outstanding productions were those in 1948, 1949, 1951 and 1959 of Lindsay's *The Three Estates*, presented again in 1973, but these productions could not be said to have generated any great response from contemporary Scottish writers. The official Festival usually presents a Scottish play, but all too often the plays chosen are such that they would never have appeared were there not the necessity to put on Scottish work of some description. The Festival Fringe has however proved a nursery for some of the most interesting contemporary Scottish writers, and although the productions may have been on occasion inadequate, at least the experimental facility, missing for so much of the time in Scotland, is available for a few weeks of the year in Edinburgh.

Such productions have often been amateur ones, and although the most interesting work has tended to be presented by the Scottish university drama groups, it is worth making the point here that although amateur activity has declined numerically since its hey-day in the inter-war period it has increased remarkably in scope so that one can find at the Scottish Community Drama Association's festivals plays not only by James Scotland or Joe Corrie being presented but also work by Beckett or Pinter or Brecht.

To sum up, Scottish theatre as a whole now offers a wider range of classical and contemporary drama to its customers and this is an obvious gain, but as far as Scottish drama is concerned it is perhaps premature to be too optimistic, yet it has to be admitted that at the moment there is more cause for optimism than there has been for some time. If the momentum which appears to have been generated since the beginning of the seventies can be maintained we could see the first real flowering of Scottish drama. Of course the right kinds of theatrical conditions do not of themselves guarantee great drama, but they are a sine qua non.

As regards the standards of theatre production in Scotland, the present writer's experience of English theatrical companies, including the two national ones, leads him to conclude that standards are generally high in Scotland and the chances of seeing a thoroughly bad performance in a Scottish theatre are low. It may well be partially a result of the overproduction of British drama schools and the consequent high unemployment rate among actors, which enables managements to pick and choose. Whatever the reason, one criticism that cannot be levelled at our Scottish theatres is that they regularly mount shoddy productions. Indeed one remembers with considerable pleasure a large number of distinguished presentations.

As far as the audiences themselves are concerned, we cannot pretend that the Scottish theatre has a steady audience upon which it can rely. Audiences fluctuate and vary from theatre to theatre, but only about half our theatres have played to over 50% capacity in recent years. Our theatres are permanently hard up, but as this is a condition of all artistic ventures in Britain, it does not call for particular comment. What is worth remarking on is the pattern of finance. All our theatres depend to some extent on public finance, whether from the Scottish Arts Council or the relevant local authority: Scottish theatres have recently tended to be subsidized in the 50 to 60 per cent region by public funds — an exception is Pitlochry, whose subsidy has never exceeded 40 per cent. A comparison with the position in English theatres shows that Scottish theatres have been drawing less proportionately of their costs from the trading revenue than English theatres, most of which recover at least 50 per cent of costs in this way, and some of which draw quite spectacular percentages from the box office by Scottish standards.

The basic reason for the large dependence on subsidy in Scotland is obvious. The theatres do not play to anything like capacity. The more they approach capacity, the higher the proportion of costs taken at the box office, and eventually the smaller will be the subvention from public funds. There is one obvious danger in a situation where a theatre is over-dependent on the public purse: it is liable to the pressures which occasionally accompany these funds, particulary local government funds. The recent history of the Citizens', for example, includes several instances of councillors angered by a production (which they may not even have seen) demanding that the Corporation grant be cut, although so far without success. Even the Lyceum in Edinburgh attracted similar criticisms from the chairman of Edinburgh District Council shortly after local government reform. The Traverse, for its part, must by now have accepted critical and at times abusive comment as a hazard of the Edinburgh scene.

The buildings which house our companies are for the most part old; Scotland did not share in the British upsurge in theatre building which gave us the Yvonne Arnaud Theatre at Guildford, the Belgrade Theatre, Coventry, the Chichester Festival Theatre and the Nottingham Playhouse. There has, nonetheless, been some theatre-building in recent years in Scotland — the multi-purpose MacRobert Centre at Stirling University, a number of small arts centre theatres, the new Byre at St. Andrews and, most recently, the Eden Court complex at Inverness which when it opened in 1976 was highly praised for the design of its auditorium. The Lyceum Company has waited in vain, however, for the theatre which was to form part of the now defunct opera house project. The Glasgow Cultural Centre, which would include a replacement for the Citizens' theatre, seems no nearer commencement and meanwhile the buildings round about the present theatre have been demolished. Dundee Repertory remains in its converted church, and the Pitlochry company is still in its original 'temporary' building. Obviously buildings do not make theatres, but the English experience tends to suggest that an exciting new building can provide a focal point in the community and lead to substantially increased audiences.

By way of counter-balance to this rather depressing picture, we must mention Scottish Opera's triumphant restoration of Glasgow's Theatre Royal, which had been in use as the head-quarters of Scottish Television since 1957 until its gala re-opening on 14 October 1975 with a production of *Die Fledermaus*. The theatre is also being used for touring companies, both operatic and dramatic.

One major development since the war is the School of Drama in Glasgow, part of the Royal Scottish College of Music and Drama. Largely the result of James Bridie's determination to set Scottish drama on its own feet, independent of the English theatre, it was opened by him in 1950 not long before his death. With its 'bilingual' system of training it enables the aspiring young Scottish actor to develop his art in such a way that he can work in either Scotland or England. It is obviously an economic necessity that the Glasgow-trained actor should have a command of Scots (as spoken now and in the past) and a feeling for Scots characters, if Scottish drama is to be adequately realised on the stage. That graduates of this college do have the necessary command and feeling is one hopeful sign for the future of Scottish drama. Among the more distinguished former students are Ian Richardson, who is noted for his acting with the Royal Shakespeare Company; Robert Kidd, who has held the post of artistic director of the Royal Court Theatre; and Denise Coffey, the actress and director.

The University of Glasgow, which contributed to the teaching of students at the Drama College from the beginning, established a drama department of its own in 1966 and now offers full honours courses. Drama teaching occupies a role of growing significance throughout Scottish education, and can take the form of practical and/or theoretical work.

As if by way of acknowledging the improving situation, a Scottish Arts Council report *Theatre in Scotland*, published in 1970, toyed with the idea of the establishment of a Scottish National Theatre, but having alluded to the difficulties that lay in the path of the National Theatre project in London the report stated:

If the repertory theatre in Scotland flourishes and
demonstrates what the living theatre can at its best
achieve, the future establishment of a National Theatre
will be greatly encouraged. But we believe that the
development of a major Scottish touring company could
also provide a basis for it.

Consequently the Lyceum company was given special financial provision, in return for which efforts have been made to encourage Scottish drama; but the major touring company is not much nearer now than it was in 1970, and perhaps that is not a great loss. A national theatre need not be either a building or a particular company; it can be the sum of the theatrical activity in the country. Indeed, special national theatre buildings and national theatre companies can act as drains on resources to the detriment of geographically dispersed theatrical activity. This would be an unfortunate consequence, particularly since the Scottish Arts Council and the local authorities have been instrumental in building up a network of arts centres and arts guilds which present a variety of dramatic and musical performances by touring companies of a high standard.

The latent interest in such tours has been amply demonstrated by the writer's own experience in North Ayrshire where until 1970 no professional performances were seen, although there was a substantial amount of amateur activity of varying quality. On this basis an arts centre was established (although without a physical centre) and five years later an average season can bring to an area with a population of less than twenty thousand an opera company, two dance companies, the 7:84 Theatre Company, the Scottish National Orchestra and a number of smaller dramatic and musical events. The centre is one of the most successful in Scotland in the promotion of professional performances, yet it started from virtually nothing only a few years ago. Such success is of course due largely to the existence of a potential audience, suitable halls and hard work by the people who run the centre, but could never have been achieved without substantial financial support from the Scottish Arts Council, and the area's local authorities. The story can be paralleled elsewhere in Scotland, in Cumbernauld, in Irvine, in Kirkcaldy, in Motherwell, where the civic centre is on a grander scale, and in Inverness where the Eden Court complex is on an even grander one — much to the chagrin of the reorganized authority which found itself faced with rapidly escalating costs.

It would be disastrous if excessive concentration on a national theatre were to harm those developments or the professional repertory theatres. The time may come for a national company, but only when theatre is established much more firmly throughout the country.

In 1969 the Scottish theatrical world was somewhat startled by a remarkable development, the publication of a new magazine *Scottish Theatre*. There have been several magazines in the past concerned with the theatre in Scotland and reference has been made to some of them: one characteristic they have tended to share is a direct association with a particular movement — *Scots Theatre* with Unity Theatre, *The Scottish Player* with the Scottish National Players, *Scottish Stage* with the amateur movement in general — whereas *Scottish Theatre* was independent of all existing theatres. Throughout its four-year existence it was edited and managed by one man, Kenneth Roy. Mr Roy's enthusiasm and energy produced not only a glossy monthly magazine which set a high standard in critical discussion of the Scottish theatre, but a play publication venture and a small touring company, the Stage Company Scotland, which presented new Scottish plays. That *Scottish Theatre* and its allied activities have come to an end is a matter for great sadness; that they survived for so long in the face of mounting financial difficulties, with very little subvention from the public purse, is a tribute to Mr Roy's determination and ability.

As a magazine *Scottish Theatre* was wide ranging in its contents. In addition to regular reviews of the month's productions in the Scottish repertory theatres, there were articles on the amateur theatre and theatrical history, critical assessments of playwrights and reports on the theatre south of the border. Running through the magazine were its editor's perceptive critical values: Mr Roy could distinguish very well between the significant and the meretricious in writing and production. He championed the cause of theatre in Scotland against what he saw as the excessive hand-outs from public funds to opera, and he championed the playwright Cecil Taylor whom he felt was neglected in his own country. It is a great pity that the magazine is not still with us and that Mr Roy's critical eye is not turned on the contemporary scene.

CHAPTER ELEVEN
Writing since the War

THE SITUATION OF THE WRITER IN SCOTLAND has changed since the Second World War with the continuing development of radio and then latterly the introduction of television. What both radio and television offer the dramatist is an extension of his market. There is a fairly steady demand for scripts of various kinds, not only 'pure' drama written specifically for either medium, but also adaptations of novels and — particularly in television — new episodes for the various series that are constantly being transmitted. Much of this work is pot-boiling, but to the writer who can establish himself it can ensure a good and regular income. He might feel that he is unable to fulfil himself as much as he could in the theatre, but he does have relative security. The Scottish writer who works for television can find himself contributing to a series which may have little to do with his principal artistic concerns, but he will have the experience of seeing his work performed.

The danger for the theatre is that dramatic writers of worth are lost because it cannot offer the same opportunities. As far as the Scottish theatre is concerned, it inevitably offers a more limited market than the English theatre. Writers therefore receive scant financial encouragement, and despite recent more hopeful signs have not yet received adequate artistic encouragement either. The result has been that a playwright, before he or she reaches maturity, may abandon theatre altogether for television, where a different kind of drama is required. Tom Wright, for example, having written the highly successful *There Was a Man* for the theatre, has turned his attention to television and radio where his work regularly appears. Unless some way is found of rewarding and encouraging young playwrights in the theatre there will be many more like him in the future.

Turning now to Scottish dramatic writing in the last thirty years, we see that what we might call the traditional Scottish play has continued to be written — that is, the play with an overtly Scottish subject, almost always historical, often using some kind of rural dialect. Exponents of this genre include Robert McLellan, whose work has already been discussed,

Alexander Reid, Alexander Scott and Robert Kemp, to whom more detailed attention will now be given.

Robert Kemp was born in 1908 on the Orkney island of Longhope, the son of a minister. He pursued a career in journalism and broadcasting in England and Scotland before turning to full-time writing in 1947. Kemp chaired the Edinburgh Gateway Company from its foundation in 1953 till 1960. He died in 1967. The most immediately obvious characteristic of his writing is that it is mainly writing of the surface, reasonably effective theatrically but lacking in any depth of dramatic motivation. His themes are varied, but there is an emphasis on the historical, particularly on the historical ecclesiastical. Like many Scots dramatists, Kemp seems to feel more sure of himself when dealing with the past than with the present. He appears to be more certain of the landmarks of Scottish history and the nature of the historical Scottish identity than he is of contemporary experience and the problems of identity it presents to the modern Scot.

Three of Kemp's full-length plays — *Festival Fever*, *The Penny Wedding* and *The Perfect Gent* — do have contemporary settings. *Festival Fever* (4 June 1956, Sherek Players in Lyceum, Edinburgh) is a light piece with incidental touches of satire set in Edinburgh during the International Festival. *The Penny Wedding* (28 October 1957, Gateway), also set in Edinburgh, satirizes the Lallans movement, personified by one of the central characters who insists in speaking this curious language despite the fact that no one can understand him. *The Perfect Gent* (30 October 1962, Gateway) is set in the Highlands and is an unpretentious little piece about bank robbers on the run.

Kemp's output of historical pieces was prolific: *The Saxon Saint* (29 August 1949, Dunfermline Abbey), specially written for performance at Dunfermline Abbey, does attempt to convey something of the intellectual conflict between the traditional Scottish ecclesiastical parties' view of things and the English approach which Margaret, wife of Duncan Canmore, sought to introduce, although the subject is not explored very well or very deeply; *Master John Knox* (10 October 1960, Gateway), which was written for the Church of Scotland to mark the fourth centenary of the Reformation, tells its story in a somewhat pedestrian fashion, although there are some effective dramatic touches; *The King of Scots* (27 August 1951, Dunfermline

Abbey) is a pageant rather than a play and, as the title implies, deals with the life of Robert the Bruce.

A Trump for Jericho, first performed as *Walls of Jericho* by the Scottish National Players at the end of their career (4 April 1947, Lanark), takes a light-hearted look at the effects of religious controversy during the period of the Disruption in the Scottish church, while *A Nest of Singing Birds* (October 1949, Gateway) deals with an eighteenth-century controversy as to just how singing in church ought to be conducted. Kemp appears to be suggesting that such disputations, which have characterised the history of the Church in Scotland, are basically foolish and better forgotten, an essentially humane and civilized twentieth-century attitude but one which does not take account of the fanaticism and cruelty which often characterized these disputations.

The Other Dear Charmer (19 November 1951, Glasgow Citizens' at Gaiety, Ayr), Kemp's best play, deals with the love affair between Mrs MacLehose and Robert Burns. Burns ultimately leaves Mrs MacLehose for Jean Armour not merely because he prefers the country girl, but also because in the play she represents the Scottish folk traditions, whereas Mrs MacLehose represents the Anglo-Scottish influence in art and life.

The conflict between the Scottish and Anglo-Scottish traditions is presented throughout the play in the progress of the relationship between Burns and Nancie or, as she prefers to put it, in the language of Augustan artifice, between Sylvander and Clarinda. Burns's final declaration against Edinburgh and Clarinda, and for Jean Armour, Scots poetry and the traditional Scottish way of life is well prepared for in the play — even while he is in Edinburgh, he has a child by an Edinburgh street girl. The conflict is resolved when Burns tells Nancie that he has bought a farm near Dumfries. Nancie protests, but Burns is adamant:

> . . . What use is your Edinburgh society to me? No, no, I'll be better there, on the moors above Dumfries, with the shades of Ferguson and Ramsay to walk beside me, and the music of country songs in my head, than here among the professors and the ministers and the lawyers . . . I'm done with Edinburgh, Nancie! I'm not a white-handed gentleman and never will be. I'm a country farmer and a

Scottish bard. And there's one more bit of news I have for
you. (*A pause*). I'm married: I've owned Jean Armour as
my wife.

Kemp presents Nancie's fate with genuine pathos, and the
characterization throughout, even of the minor characters such
as the Puritan bigot, the Reverend Kemp, is far more convincing
than in most of Kemp's other work.

Alexander Reid has had success with two plays written in
Scots — *The Lass Wi' the Muckle Mou* and *The Warld's
Wonder*. Both plays are set in the Borders at the end of the
Middle Ages. Reid has attempted to write about the modern
world, for example in *Diana* and *The Wax Doll*; the first deals
with a poltergeist in a Highland manse and seeks to explore
the darker side of human nature, while the second has as its
subject matter faith healing. Neither play is particularly successful and we can only regret that the flair for wit and satire found
in Reid's Scots comedies has never been applied to the
contemporary scene.

Alexander Scott has had several plays performed, the best
of which is probably *Right Royal*, an amusing period piece
revolving round the roguish King Dod of Fife.

Another genre is what we could call the modern Scots play,
that is the play which attempts to come to grips with contemporary Scottish life and seeks to recreate the patterns of
urban speech. There are no outstanding dramatists in this genre,
for none of the writers concerned has ever developed as we might
have hoped, and in some cases, still hope, they will. But one who
does merit further attention is George Munro.

He was born in Govan in 1901 and died in Ayrshire in 1968.
Most of his professional life was spent in London as a journalist,
but his plays are very much concerned with the West of Scotland
as he knew it as a boy and as a young man. Munro's family was
a Christian Brethren one, and in all four of the plays to be
discussed here the Brethren figure to some extent. As the West
of Scotland is obsessed by religious bigotry and football, the one
closely connected to the other, so Munro returns constantly to
these subjects.

Gold in His Boots (27 January 1947, Unity in Queen's Theatre,
Glasgow) tells the story of the rise of Tommy Craig in the world
of professional football. Tommy comes from the obscurity of
Miners' Row in Clanmarnock, where his father is without a job

and his mother is a dedicated member of the Brethren, but the world he enters is seen to be a sordid one where players are bought and sold like carcases. So Tommy ultimately abandons first-class football (after a last marvellous game) to marry his childhood sweetheart. Munro brings out well both the harshness of life in Miners' Row, where football is an obsession and a potential escape route, and the crude commercialism of the world of first-class football. It is an interesting play although there is too much reliance on contrivances of plot, the characterization is not always convincing, and there is some irrelevant griping about the relationship between Scotland and England.

Vineyard Street (10 October 1949, Glasgow Citizens') is set in a Brethren milieu in the small west coast town of Nineveh — which shows striking similarities to Stevenston in north Ayrshire, the part of the world where Munro was brought up. Mary McIsaac, daughter of a leading light in the local tabernacle, Bethseda Hall, imagines herself visited by the Lord at a Hogmanay meeting. She conceives a child — on Holy Isle, off Arran — and insists that it is a child of God, whereas the father is really Heuck Hogarth, a local sailor who has been her suitor for a long time. Heuck, whose father is also a member of the Brethren, catches Mary in a spiritual trance as she offers herself to the Lord — Munro here conveys very well the overlap of spirituality and sexuality. Heuck supposedly drowns and Mary brings up her son, Emmanuel, to be an evangelist. On his twenty-first birthday — again significantly Hogmanay — Heuck returns, contrives to make the boy drunk and, it is implied, thus saves him from his fate. Heuck and Mary are rather unconvincingly reconciled.

The strength of the play lies in Munro's ability to convey the claustrophobic feeling of the Brethren world, its narrowness, its meanness, its hypocrisy, and its obsession with hell and death (Moses McIsaac, Mary's father, is appropriately an undertaker). He also catches well the petty rivalries of Bethseda Hall, which mock all its pretensions to virtue. The characterization is not black and white, but much more rounded than in *Gold in His Boots*. Some of the plot is a little contrived, in particular the death and return of Heuck. Furthermore, since Munro is dealing with people who take themselves very seriously indeed, there is a risk at times of bathos which he does not always manage to avoid.

Mark But This Flea (2 March 1970, Arts Theatre Group, University of Glasgow) was never properly finished and was unperformed when its author died. The theme is the destruction wrought by sectarian bigotry. In present-day Nineveh Benny Lomax is attracted to a Catholic girl, Nan Brogan, and forsakes his career as a Brethren preacher, as he had previously forsaken football for the Brethren. The play concentrates on the reaction of Benny's family, culminating in ultimate rejection. As a development of his central theme, Munro shows the havoc sectarianism, and in some ways religion itself, have wreaked in other characters' lives, for example on the life of Valiant, an alcoholic lapsed Catholic, and on the lives of Benny's parents. The play obviously needed the revision its dying author was unable to give it, for it is uneven and unbalanced. Munro's faults — turgid dialogue, over-use of literary quotations, a tendency to hector his audience about side issues — are all there, but might well have disappeared in a redraft.

Gay Landscape (24 February 1958, Glasgow Citizens') is Munro's best play. It ranges over several decades in the life of the Gascoyne family, originally Highland but now belonging to Govan. There are three acts in the play, each separated by a number of years. On three occasions — the funeral of their father, the christening of Martha Gascoyne's illegitimate child, and the funeral of their mother — all the members of the family gather and give rein to the hatred which unites them. This hatred appears at first to stem from particular causes, but closer examination shows it to be congenital and related to the environment the family have grown up in — the industrial area of Clydeside. At the christening of Martha's child several of the Gascoyne sisters talk about the Clyde:

MARTHA   I've walked Clydeside at daybreak and
mirkest hour. I've studied it in storm and sun. Buildings
and wharves and stocks move into skyline setting for me.
I've felt tender for the tracery of tenements touched by
sun or winter cloudbank. But it's an eye below my
seeing eye; and alien eye; that's taking it all in.

ANNE: That's your hieland eye. For we're alien. We're
no tenement trash. It was glen and mountain side, not
close stairs and tenement gullies we were born to tread.
(*In rage, she goes to the window*) That sheuch was never

meant to croon our cradle song. Clearer water
should've made the lullaby we heard. We opened our
eyes to clatter, batter, bash and blistering shriek.
(*Swings on her heels. Comes down CENTRE almost to
the floats*) There's times when he's climbing the pulpit
ahint the beadle, that I'd like to take a grip of Ian
Alastair's coat-tails. (*Oracularly*) "Ye men of Clyde," I'd
say, "Unplug your ears. Strip the blinkers from your
eyes. When you chitter nonsense about the bonnie banks
o' Clyde, unfankle your teeth: Clyde built! Roamin' in
the gloaming! Take another look. You'll maybe tell
yourselves the truth then. A stretching stream has
worked on you a patriotism that's a world's wonder. If
only it'd suck all of you into its maw, calamity'd be
complete. From Falls of Clyde to Tail o' the Bank it
works nothing but destruction. Destruction. Dirt.
Despair. Grappling with it men become Masters of Men.
But never Masters of You." Mother Clyde! I hate you.

All the sisters have or have had an ambivalent attitude to
the Clyde: it has at times seemed to offer the possibility of
happiness; but more often it has meant hardness and misery. For
John Gascoyne their father it has been the failure of the promise
it held out to him. It has steeled the heart of all his family. Anne
in particular regards the Gascoynes as alien in Clydeside: they
belong in the Highlands. Munro is not allowing his characters to
indulge in rustic escapism here, but attempting to mirror the
effects of the migrations to Glasgow from the Highlands that
have taken place for the last hundred and fifty years. Life has
turned sour for the Gascoynes, and it is Clydeside that is held
responsible by Munro. The exterior landscape is mirrored in the
family, not only in the hatred, but in the sordidness of its life.
Drunkenness and incest are prominent in the play, reminding
the most socially aspirant of the Gascoynes what the city has
really made of them. The texture of the writing, as can be seen,
is dense. Munro throughout his work uses highly figurative
language to heighten feeling, and succeeds best in this play.
Gay Landscape is a grim play but a successful one, which makes
a powerful statement about the West of Scotland and recreates
that region's life vividly and imaginatively.

Munro's contribution to the Scottish theatre was an attempt
to move it towards coming to grips with Scottish urban

experience. The only sad feature of his work is that while we can accept the truth of his vision, nonetheless its narrowness proves a limitation. We can only wish that he had moved beyond his own deeply-felt experience of sectarianism and football more often.

Scottish drama had rather a lean period in the sixties and is only just recovering from it, so there is something of a gap between the writers just discussed and more recent ones. The present recovery does however seem to be an encouraging one. We now have a number of interesting writers working in Scotland from whom substantial and more mature work can still be expected. Furthermore, they are writers who have not in any way restricted themselves to one genre or another as Kemp and Munro tended to; they move with relative ease between the historical and the modern naturalistic form and along the way encompass other forms altogether.

Mention was made earlier of two writers who have been closely associated with the Traverse Theatre — Stanley Eveling and Cecil Taylor. Eveling is a northern Englishman, a philosopher by profession, who has had theatrical success both in Scotland and beyond. It has to be said that his concerns are not particularly Scottish, nor are the settings of his plays. Eveling is very much a writer who operates internationally, in that his themes, while they could be construed as Scottish, can just as readily be related to English or continental experience.

Eveling can be regarded as a writer concerned with personal and political morality, for all that the language and the action in some of his work have attracted abuse in the form of accusations of immorality. His view of modern life is rather a bleak and pessimistic one and at times critics have indicated impatience with the incessant repetition of this view. In form he ranges widely from the surrealism of *The Lunatic, The Secret Sportsman and the Woman Next Door*, an initially rather puzzling work in which the author explores the deeper implications of sexual fantasy, to the naturalism of *Come and Be Killed. Come and Be Killed* (13 July 1967, Traverse) presents us with a fashionably permissive and free-thinking young man, Jim, who seduces a casual girl-friend, Bettina, then arranges an abortion for her to deal with the consequences of that seduction. Bettina, in an effective theatrical gesture, brings Jim face to face with the reality of the abortion by informing him on her return from having it performed that there is a present for him in her bag. Jim puts his hand into Bettina's bag and draws it out again covered in blood. It is in fact the blood of a dead rabbit. "Ours," she tells Jim, "was smaller."

Cecil Taylor is a writer very different in kind from Eveling, and his connection with the Traverse is less close. Taylor, who comes from a Glasgow Jewish background, works from an English base and since he began writing, his work (which has been prolific) has appeared not only in the theatre in Scotland and south of the border but also at frequent intervals on television. One suspects that Taylor in some ways feels neglected in his native country, and indeed there is evidence to support such a view. This neglect is a great pity, for Taylor has a great deal to say about Scotland that is worth hearing. Above all he acts as a necessary antidote to what he himself has called "The Scots tradition of the self-congratulatory play" to which he feels the Lyceum Company in Edinburgh has been committed.

The theme to which Taylor returns repeatedly is the failure of socialism. Many of his characters, from the hilarious would-be revolutionaries of *Allergy* to the old, defeated socialist hero of *Bloch's Play*, illustrate all too well this failure. He scrupulously avoids in his work the kind of mawkish sentimentality that now surrounds the presentation in the theatre of Red Clydeside as much as it used to surround the presentation of rural Scotland. In *Allergy* (18 January 1966, Traverse) Jim, the editor of a somewhat obscure left-wing journal of limited circulation, has retired to a cottage in Ross-shire to write a definitive work, 'Twentieth-Century Marxism — An Enquiry'. At his lonely cottage arrive Christopher, who contributes to Jim's paper under a nom de plume while earning his living as a local newspaper reporter, and Barbara, 'regular contributor to the *Daily Worker* fighting fund'. It is clear that these two intend to have an affair and propose to use Jim's cottage to initiate it. It is a perfect situation for Taylor to satirize the ineffectiveness, sectarianism and plain silliness of the Left and he does not miss his opportunity. The play takes on farcical overtones when it emerges that Christopher, who is married, is allergic to adultery and as a consequence has developed a hideous rash. This is too much for Barbara and the play ends with Christopher departing for Glasgow and Jim and Barbara climbing into bed together.

Bread and Butter (7 July 1966, Jeanetta Cochrane Theatre,

London) likewise illustrates human failings in the bearers of the revolutionary torch. The play traces the lives of Alex and Morris, two Glasgow Jews, from the thirties to the present day. Morris continually dreams and speculates about the advance of socialism and time after time his political judgements are shown to be wildly inaccurate. Finally he abandons his rather self-righteous pose and admits that his life adds up to nothing: nothing has been achieved. He is no longer capable of even a token gesture of defiance and can only seek consolation — as in fact he has done throughout — in extra-marital sex. Alex, on the other hand, while sharing his friend Morris's views, has tended to concentrate more on building as tolerable a life as possible: he and his wife buy a little flat in Gorbals, and when they have a windfall they ignore Morris's suggestion that they should all go off to Israel but decide that from then on they will spend half of the year on holiday in Dunoon. However, for Alex too life has turned somewhat sour: his wife dies of pleurisy and he is left alone with his dog. But Alex has the ability to take pleasure in small things, feeding the pigeons or listening to the chaffinches singing in Queen's Park. It is a moving and saddening play which suggests all too clearly that the possibilities of life are limited and that dreams can be futile and even dangerous. But Taylor never seems to give up hope totally. As Alex says to Morris towards the end of the play: "You're needed, Morris, to keep the picture of what could be alive and in front of people, to keep pushing them, to keep banging and banging at the door, until at last it breaks open".

The Traverse was responsible for the premiere of Stewart Conn's one-act play *The King* which shows the influence of writers like Pinter and the Theatre of the Absurd movement. It is, in fact, not typical of the author's work. Conn occupies a central position in the Scottish theatre today not merely because he is slowly establishing a body of work worthy of respect, but also because of his position as the BBC's senior radio drama producer. Radio drama offers writers the chance to do original work and to have their theatre plays adapted for transmission. Such opportunities have in recent years been much more substantial in radio than in television which more and more has concentrated on adaptations of novels and on series. This is not to deny the worth of much of what emanates from Queen Margaret Drive — for example, the adaptation of *Sunset Song*

— but simply to point out the facts. The appointment of Roderick Graham as Head of TV Drama at BBC Scotland in 1976 may, however, lead to a clear change of direction towards original rather than adapted material. The contribution to drama by the major commercial company, Scottish Television, remains insubstantial. Thus, at the moment of writing, dramatists for the most part look to Stewart Conn's department for work outside the theatre. And from both Conn and his associate, Gordon Emslie, they have received an encouragement not often found in the live theatre.

In his own writing Conn has produced naturalistic drama with a contemporary background, for example *I didn't always live here* (18 April 1967, Citizens'), which explores the relationships between two Glasgow women, one working-class, one genteel but down on her luck, and at times in performance seemed more of a documentary than a play. In *The Aquarium* (8 May 1973, Lyceum) he examines the tensions between the members of a lower middle class family at a point where they have become mutually destructive. It is a play at times reminiscent of the work of Arthur Miller, and it has dramatic power and compassion. At times one does feel, however, that the script requires more work by its author, that the play's potential is more substantial than its actual achievement.

Conn has also turned his attention to Scottish history in *The Burning* (18 November 1971, Lyceum), but it is a much bleaker view of the past than that presented by many of the dramatists we have discussed earlier. *The Burning* is set, like Robert McLellan's *Jamie the Saxt*, during the period of James's reign before the Union of the Crowns, but while in McLellan's play the king appears as a canny, sympathetic character afflicted by intriguing nobles, in *The Burning* he is presented as a shabby, even cowardly, figure not above infliction of terrible cruelty if it serves his political and religious beliefs. Conn tells us that the play "did not spring from any predisposition on my part towards Scots historical drama; but from what struck me as the theatrical potential of the theme, and its relevance today". The play examines the relationship between the king and Francis Hepburn, Earl of Bothwell, who seeks to usurp James I's throne. In the furtherance of this aim Bothwell enlists the aid of 'witches'. When they are arrested he leaves them to their fate while he forces the king at the point of his sword to restore the titles and lands of which James had stripped him. This 'reconciliation' is of no help to the innocent victims who have been caught up in the hunt for the agents of the devil, for by now they have been burnt at the stake after being tortured to the point of confession.

At the end of the play Bothwell remarks to James: "We are the upper and nether millstones, you and I. One way or another, it is those trapped in the middle must pay the price". The events of the play have, of course, borne out this epigrammatic utterance; but one could wish that the playwright had concentrated more on the politics and, indeed, on the psychology of superstition than he does. Much of the action is concerned with the witch-hunting and interrogations, and while the scenes have power and theatricality, these qualities stem from the subject portrayed rather than from any very substantial infusion of energy by the dramatist. Indeed it is a play that tells a story at the expense of exploring fully its implications. It is however a story well told and put across with a skilful avoidance of the linguistic trap: Conn suggests the Scots language of the time by rhythm and by a skilful though sparing use of archaism.

Hector MacMillan has also turned to history for his material, as, for example, the visit of George the Fourth to Edinburgh in *The Royal Visit* and the hopeless 'insurrection' of 1820 in *The Rising*. In *The Gay Gorbals* (12 February 1976, Traverse) he tackles a contemporary theme — the position of the homosexual in Scottish society, a society where the law still regards relations between members of the same sex as criminal. It is a very lively piece of theatre, although the basic theme does tend to get buried in an extravaganza of character and action.

In MacMillan's work one finds commitment to socialism, a commitment which lacks the ironic self-awareness associated with Cecil Taylor. Indeed, the overt call for the workers of the world to unite at the end of his most commercially successful play *The Sash* (13 August 1973, Pool Theatre, Edinburgh, as part of the Festival Fringe) is embarassing. *The Sash*, has, however, the great merit of dealing with an aspect of recognizable Scottish experience which has not been given as much attention as it deserves, namely the conflict between Catholic and Protestant. It is a vigorous, raw work which makes up for in energy what it lacks in depth. The rawness is found not only in the behaviour of the central character, Bill MacWilliam, a dedicated Orangeman, but in language which is sometimes as coarse as that used by the kind of people MacMillan is seeking to represent on stage. We need not be prudes to have some misgivings about such dialogue, for if dramatists are simply to reproduce actual speech rather than to create the illusion of how people talk, then we are in for some extremely dreich evenings indeed.

Similar misgivings arise from a consideration of Bill Bryden's *Willie Rough* (10 February 1972, Lyceum), which achieved a great success at its first performance. It is not hard to account for this: it had a cast of some of the finest Scottish actors in the business, professionals able to invest the most banal dialogue with undeserved significance, and the subject was Red Clydeside, very topical with the UCS work-in still fresh in mind. One suspects that the misguided sentimentality which insisted that ships must be built on the Clyde, whether anyone wished to buy them at the economic price or not, attached itself to this play and judged it to be a great work. It is in truth rather a mundane account of a Greenock shipyard strike during the First World War. The main characters — Willie Rough, the naive union man who is only interested in helping his fellows, and Charlie McGrath, the supposed revolutionary who in fact is after a comfortable job in the union — have overmuch of the stereotype about them. The language, as in *The Sash*, abounds in the obscenities beloved of the West of Scotland, thereby making any depth of expression difficult to achieve.

Bryden's *Benny Lynch* (1 March 1974, Lyceum) is a more satisfactory work because, although the action is played out against a background of poverty and deprivation that cries out for comment, the dramatist is content for most of the time to allow the comment to emerge from his narration. Benny Lynch was a Gorbals boy who rose from the boxing booths to become world flyweight champion in the 1930s. Unfortunately, for all his astounding grace in the ring Lynch succumbed to the sordid excesses present in his background and over-indulged to such an extent that he lost his title. From then on he degenerated, finally dying in a Glasgow hospital in 1946, having been carried in from the streets. He was thirty-three years old.

The story of Lynch's life is one of terrible pathos, if not perhaps tragedy, and Bryden relates it in a succession of fifteen scenes with an avoidance of sentimentality. He conveys with skill the world of the slum lad who has made the big time and cannot quite believe that he is one of the stars whom small boys and grown men adulate. The play reminds one of George Munro's *Gold in his Boots*, although Bryden, constrained by historical fact, has a less romantic ending. His treatment of the world of professional sport is also different from Munro's: whereas professional football is presented by Munro as peopled by rogues and sharks eager to exploit young talent, Bryden suggests that the relationship between Benny and his trainers is for the most part built on their admiration for his remarkable talents.

While at the Lyceum Bryden encouraged the actor Roddy McMillan to write *The Bevellers* (16 February 1973, Lyceum). McMillan had written nothing since *All in Good Faith* in 1958, a play of urban working-class life. *The Bevellers* is again very much proletarian drama, reflecting perhaps McMillan's own life before he became an actor, and his involvement with Unity Theatre in Glasgow. It is set in the bevelling shop of a Glasgow glassworks and, observing the classical unities, relates the experiences of a new apprentice on his first day of work. Norrie Beaton is just a boy, a fact emphasised by his constant references to the school he has left, and is ill-prepared for the harshness and cruelty he encounters in the bevelling shop. For all the occasional interventions of a kindly foreman, Norrie is thoroughly brutalised by the end of his first day, as a result of the behaviour of the bevellers, in particular the Rouger, whose character verges on the grotesque. It is a grim play which allows little scope for optimism, as it mirrors the all too prevalent barbarism of Scottish life. The author's obvious humanity and concern do little to lighten the gloom. It is a powerful work and one looks to McMillan to explore more deeply the behaviour he has so accurately documented.

There are other writers not so far dealt with who perhaps ought to be mentioned, in particular Joan Ure, whose plays have a delicacy and an irony whose very fastidiousness may have prevented her work receiving more recognition, and Tom Gallacher who has made a reputation beyond Scotland as much as in it, particularly with his play *Mr Joyce is Leaving Paris* (16 March 1971, Eblana Theatre, Dublin). Gallacher's debut in the professional theatre in Scotland, *Our Kindness to Five Persons* was unfortunately marred by very bad casting and production. Gallacher appears to have a penchant for 'literary' plays: his

Revival! for example, has as its central character an actor about to play the part of Solness in Ibsen's *The Masterbuilder* and *Sea Change* is a reworking of *The Tempest*. *Mr Joyce is Leaving Paris* is not dissimilar: it is in two acts, the first of which presents the Irish writer James Joyce living in poverty in Trieste in 1908 and sponging off his brother Stanislaus, and the second of which presents us with the successful Joyce in Paris in 1939 assailed by voices from his past which accuse him of using, and in the process, of destroying other human beings in the interests of his art. It is a clever and skilful piece that explores in a stimulating fashion the relationship between the artist and his materials. Gallacher has recently been extremely well served by the Scottish theatre in contrast to his earlier experiences. The Pitlochry Festival Theatre in particular has presented his work regularly. He is a dramatist who by his own admission is not fashionable: he has no interest in the ordinary run of the mill characters who people the plays to be seen on television, for which medium he does not write. Tom Gallacher is interested in exceptional people and builds his plays around such people.

Looking at the contemporary scene then one sees variety, but above all one sees at last Scottish dramatists as a group confronting the urban industrial experience, in stark contrast to the situation between the wars and indeed after the war: Bryden, Conn, Hector MacMillan, Roddy McMillan, C. P. Taylor, the 7:84 Company are all doing so to some extent. The quality of writing that we would want has yet to be achieved, but we are much nearer to it than we have ever been. Our writers have found the themes they need; soon they should find the concomitant maturity of style.

Pressure for the presentation of contemporary Scottish drama has increased lately. Indeed at the time of writing one is conscious of far more than at any time in the last fifteen years. It is coming from the Scottish Arts Council, to some extent from audiences (although that battle is not yet completely won) and from the playwrights themselves who in 1974 set up the Scottish Society of Playwrights to act as a ginger group and to facilitate the performance of new work through workshop sessions and by other methods.

The Scottish Arts Council, for its part, supports new writing in various ways. Grants are made to theatres putting on Scottish work, bursaries are offered to dramatists and financial support given to the Society of Playwrights mentioned above. Perhaps not all of these methods of support are equally valuable and while one could not quibble at production grants, and would welcome the support given the playwrights' organisation, bursaries to individuals are rather a different matter. Where such bursaries are recompense for work done — added income on top of meagre box office returns — the Arts Council is doing its best to remedy one of the deficiencies in the Scottish theatre referred to several times in this book. What are more difficult to accept are the ex gratia payments to deserving cases, a practice by no means confined to dramatists. A non-elected body engaging in this kind of activity is laying itself open to accusations of partiality, no matter how stringent its selection process. It would be better to concentrate on improving opportunities for production of Scottish plays and their publication, activities which are of course undertaken by the Council at the moment.

All of this pressure will not of itself produce great plays, but it should certainly help, provided that it is sustained in the face of inevitable disappointments.

CHAPTER TWELVE

Conclusion

THIS BOOK HAS BEEN CONCERNED with the attempts to develop theatrical activity and a native dramatic tradition in Scotland — in effect to create a Scottish national theatre. These attempts can be viewed as the assertion of a separate identity: throughout there has been a desire to cut free of the dominance of the English theatre in general and the London theatre in particular. This desire was articulated on several occasions, for example in the Press towards the end of the nineteenth century and by Alfred Wareing when he embarked on the Royalty venture at the beginning of this century.

Coupled with the desire to be free of the dominance of London, there has been a constant desire for 'Scottishness' in the drama. This longing for a drama that bears some relation to Scottish life is ever apparent and is to be found in the stated objects of almost all the theatrical ventures which we have considered. This longing has not, of course, been confined to the drama, but is also to be found throughout the arts during the period concerned.

In the drama the Irish experience, a tangible example of what it was hoped could be achieved, was often invoked — by Wareing, by the Scottish National Players and latterly by Unity Theatre. Retrospectively, it can be sadly observed that the achievements of the Irish and Scottish theatres differ greatly in scale. Of course the two societies were very different, Scotland being industrial while Ireland was not, Ireland undergoing a radical political upheaval which Scotland has not (although the situation may soon change).

And the problems in Scotland were enormous. The lack of theatrical and dramatic traditions made it difficult both to increase facilities, despite the brief upsurge before the onslaught of the cinema, and to develop native talent. In a situation where the London-orientated commercial theatre dominated, it fell largely to amateur groups to develop the native theatre in Scotland until, that is, the establishment of repertory theatres. There can be no denying the effort and enthusiasm of many of the amateurs whose work has been considered in the foregoing, but equally there can be no denying that at times they showed limited imagination and excessive caution, to both of which characteristics the ultimate failure of the Scottish National Players can partially be attributed. It would, however, be wrong to underestimate the contribution the amateurs made to building up the theatre in Scotland. Without their pioneering it is doubtful whether the present pattern of repertory theatres would exist. Without their development of native talent among actors and writers, there would have been nothing to build on.

What then has been achieved in the last eighty years or so? How far have we progressed towards a national theatre?

We now have a reasonable number of repertory theatres presenting varied programmes on a regular basis, although none of them has a financial situation that could honestly be described as healthy. But they survive. The Scottish playgoer is infinitely richer than he was at the beginning of the century. We also have native actors trained in Scotland and capable of establishing themselves both in their own country and elsewhere. We do not, however, have a very impressive range of dramatic achievement.

In attempting to answer the question as to why there has been no thriving drama in Scotland we are placed in the very difficult position of explaining an absence, which is much harder than explaining a presence. It would be relatively easy to trace the observable factors which led to the growth of a powerful Scottish drama had there been such a growth; seeking an explanation for its non-appearance is a much more tendentious activity.

Firstly there has been the problem of economics. We are never going to see large numbers of Scottish writers unless it is possible for them to make a living from the theatre. It is doubtful if that has ever been the case in Scotland. Barrie made his money in London, and Bridie, for all that he was based in Scotland, relied very heavily on the West End audiences and those further afield; indeed, for all his Scottishness, he worked within standard metropolitan theatrical forms. If by way of example we consider the stage history of the works of three of the important dramatists in Scotland this century who were writing primarily for the Scottish theatre, it becomes clear that none of them could have made a great deal of money from the stage. Robert McLellan has had his works performed in Scottish theatres but a total of less than twenty professional productions of twelve plays in forty years is disappointing; Robert Kemp, with almost fifty productions, has done better but he had to write twenty-five plays to achieve that number of productions; George Munro has done worst of all with each of his four plays having had one professional production only (a fifth play of Munro's was given a London production).

If a theatre is going to support writers, then it is imperative that their major works are performed again and again. It is destructive of talent that the only way in which a writer can draw a tolerable income is continually to write new plays as Kemp most obviously had to do. Even with an income from broadcasting, writing plays in Scotland this century has not been a very profitable business. If a regional writer is to succeed financially he must aim beyond the region at London and indeed at the world, and therein lies the problem; for what might be acceptable in Scotland is not necessarily so in London, a situation seen most clearly with McLellan's work. It could be argued that the writers mentioned above were simply poor writers compared to the brilliance of Bridie. Of course they were not as good, but they were also trying to do something different, which could only be done on a developing basis in the Scottish theatre. Regional theatre is only going to be acceptable in the metropolitan theatre when it reaches maturity. A metropolitan theatre may tolerate apprentice metropolitan work, but not lame plays from regional writers.

Then there is the problem of the models available to writers in the Scottish theatre this century. After Shaw and the play of ideas, the model from south of the border for much of the period under consideration was that of the light West End play, a model of little use to most writers seeking to come to grips with Scottish experience. Again Bridie could use it, for it suited his urbane and elusive dramatic persona, but other writers could not.

At home there was the model of the music-hall sketch, and many of the plays we have looked at show evidence of having been based on that model, to their detriment; for a music-hall sketch is essentially light and superficial. Furthermore in Scotland it tends to be allied to a mawkish sentimentality personified best in the work of Harry Lauder, a man of undoubted talent and inventiveness whose ultimate influence on the cultural forms of his nation has been baleful nonetheless.

Viewed from the standpoint of the present the obvious model for the Scottish dramatist in the early part of this century was Ibsen, for he was writing about a very similar kind of society, an oppressive Puritan one whose essential quality was hypocrisy; one remembers the ironic remark derived from some dialogue of Bridie's that Ibsen's real name was Henry Gibson and he came from Motherwell. Unfortunately the very Puritanism and hypocrisy on which Ibsen thrived may have served to prevent a similar dramatic awakening in Scotland if, for example, we read aright the behaviour of the Scottish National Players over *Soutarness Water*. Only a committed professional theatre would have been strong enough to overcome that kind of diffidence.

So the Scottish dramatist fell back on the music-hall sketch and the West End play as models, and he looked over his shoulder to the Irish theatre, oblivious of the fact that the Irish plays arose out of a peasant society completely different from Scottish society. The refusal to face up to the industrial experience characterizes much of the drama we have been looking at and it is not peculiar to the drama. It has been suggested that this kailyard view of Scottish experience grew out of a desire to escape the horrors of the aftermath of the industrial revolution and expresses a kind of yearning for an arcadian rural society. Certainly it is a view of experience which permeates Scottish culture, high and low. Perhaps also its development owes something to the problem of identity. After all, the best way to express Scottishness is to assert those aspects of the national identity which differentiate its people most from the rest of Britain, which very often means the Highland experience, usually embroidered and distorted. So we have the split between the real Lowland/urban experience and the fanciful rural/Highland experience, the classic case of national schizophrenia.

In the drama this schizophrenia was compounded by a fatal tendency to write about the past. Again, if you are unsure of your national identity as part of Britain, it is best asserted by revivifying a past when the nation was politically independent and people spoke a distinct tongue of their own. Before you know it, you are writing in an antiquated and obscure language about an antiquated and obscure way of life.

In the inter-war period these factors were probably aggravated by the dominance of the Community Drama Movement which, whatever its good points — and these have been referred to — was essentially concerned with generating dramatic activity within communities many of which were relatively small and non-urban, and hence more receptive to the couthy play with a rural setting than to the more radical urban play.

Since the Union, Scottish writers have become progressively more unsure of themselves and of their own identity. This is simply a facet of the problem of the one-sided relationship between the regions and the centre of power. If we have a situation where most of the power in the country is concentrated in the south of England then it is to be expected that the major cultural institutions will be situated there too and will suck in talent on the one hand and propagate the idea that their products are superior on the other. Deficiencies in the broadcasting services and the Press in Scotland are commonly attributed to such a situation. This is not necessarily to argue for home rule, but simply to point out that a dominant centre of power has the twin effects of siphoning off talent and of creating a feeling of diffidence, a lack of self-confidence elsewhere in the country. The region stops believing in its own ability to do anything as well as it is done in London.

The Scottish dramatist has therefore been in a very difficult situation, lacking outlets for both apprentice and mature work, and lacking the opportunity to build a secure financial base in his own country. Perhaps too he has been confused about the very idea of Scottish drama. Do we mean by that term 'plays written in Scotland' regardless of by whom or what they are about? Do we mean 'plays written by Scots' wherever they may live? Or 'plays about Scotland' regardless of the nationality of the writer? The underlying assumption in this book has been that Scottish drama is drama which reflects life in Scotland and has the Scottish theatre as a base for performance. As one would assume that French drama, for example, reflects French life and is performed much of the time in the French theatre. The place of residence of the writer is neither here nor there; what matters firstly is the relationship of the drama to the society and secondly, since plays cannot have a real existence outside the theatre, where it is performed.

The writers we have been considering have sought to express something of the nature of life in our society, and much of their work has been performed in Scotland. Where they have been least successful is in bridging the aesthetic and physical gaps between the local and the universal. Only a few Scottish plays have achieved recognition beyond Scotland because only a few have deserved it. The local has so often become the parochial: an excessively Scottish drama is in the end an unsatisfactory drama. Concentration on the parochial has been linked to a rather dogged attachment to naturalism, which means that few plays or scenes set off the reverberations in the mind that a writer like Chekhov can achieve within the bounds of naturalism with such apparent ease. Few Scottish dramatists have shown the capacity to move from documentation to metaphor, and it has been a crippling weakness in their work. Some have — one thinks, for example, of Bridie's *The Queen's Comedy* and Taylor's *Bread and Butter*. All too often, however, Scottish dramatists have been content simply to document and particularize. If there is to be progress in Scottish dramatic writing it is in this area that it must come.

We can anticipate with reasonable confidence the further expansion of theatrical facilities in Scotland, but cannot be so sure about the development of our drama. Neil Gunn suggested in 1938 that great drama came from a sense of national conflict or travail. Could it be that Scotland is about to enter such a period — a rediscovery of the Scottish national identity, to which devolution may lead, bringing about a rejuvenation of the creative arts? If it does we can look forward to a Scottish drama which casts off its obsessions with the past and with turgid social realism and begins to explore the deeper and more fundamental areas of experience which it has only so far touched on. Then we will have a Scottish drama worthy of respect both within Scotland and, equally importantly, in the world beyond.

SELECT BIBLIOGRAPHY

THERE ARE NOT A VERY LARGE NUMBER of books available on the Scottish theatre and the list that follows is reasonably comprehensive. For much of the research on which this book is based I was heavily reliant on periodicals, newspapers, pamphlets and collections of theatrical programmes. I have here attempted to list the principal sources of my material in the hope that any reader who wished to pursue a study of the Scottish theatre might thus be enabled to take a few short cuts.

PRE-TWENTIETH CENTURY

P. Baxter *The Drama in Perth* Perth, 1907.

W. Baynham *The Glasgow Stage* Glasgow, 1892.

J. C. Dibdin *Annals of the Edinburgh Stage* Edinburgh, 1888.

D. MacKenzie *Scotland's First National Theatre* Edinburgh, 1963.

A. J. Mill *Mediaeval Plays in Scotland* Edinburgh, 1927.

A. Robertson *History of the Dundee Theatre* London, 1949.

T. Tobin *Plays by Scots 1660-1800* Iowa, 1974.

TWENTIETH CENTURY

W. Isaac *Alfred Wareing* Green Bank Press, London, 1951.

W. Bannister *James Bridie and his Theatre* Rockcliff, London, 1955.

U. Gerber *James Bridie's Dramen* Bern, 1961.

H. Luyben *James Bridie: Clown and Philosopher* Univ. of Pennsylvania, 1965.

A. Mackie *The Scotch Comedians* Edinburgh, 1973.

The Scottish National Theatre Glasgow, 1953.

The Twelve Seasons of the Gateway Company Edinburgh, 1965.

PERIODICALS, NEWSPAPERS, PAMPHLETS AND PROGRAMMES

The following are the main magazines carrying reviews of productions and articles dealing with aspects of Scottish theatre: *The Glasgow Harlequin*, *The Northern Review*, *The Scots Magazine*, *Scots Theatre*, *Scottish Stage*, *Scottish Theatre*, *SMT Magazine*. The *Glasgow Herald* and *The Scotsman* also carry occasional reviews and features, and in the inter-war period many evening newspapers gave extensive coverage to the drama, in particular to amateur drama. All the specialist theatre magazines are no longer in existence, but back numbers of some of them, as well as past programmes and press cuttings, are available for reference in the Mitchell Library and Baillie's Library, Glasgow and Edinburgh Public Library.

NOTE ON THE TEXT OF PLAYS

AS INDICATED IN THE TEXT a considerable number of the plays performed in the Scottish theatre this century were published in book form. It should be added however that many were not, and that sometimes the work of a particular dramatist is available mainly in manuscript form. What follows is a guide to the availability of most of the plays dealt with in the text.

GLASGOW REPERTORY THEATRE
Many of the plays referred to were published by Gowans and Gray of London and Glasgow.

THE INTER-WAR PERIOD
Robert McLellan's plays have had a variety of publishers. William McLellan of Glasgow has served him well, while more recently Calder and Boyars have published *Jamie the Saxt* and *The Hypocrite*. Other of his plays remain in manuscript available from the playwright's agent.

THE SCOTTISH NATIONAL PLAYERS
John Brandane's work was published largely by Constable, while George Reston Malloch had less success in finding publishers: *Soutarness Water* was the only full-length play of his to appear from Gowans and Gray. Most of the other plays referred to were published by the Glasgow publishers Brown Son and Ferguson, W. Wilson and Co., and Gowans and Gray.

JAMES BRIDIE
Constable published virtually all of Bridie's plays.

POST-WAR WRITERS
Robert Kemp has had his work published by the St. Giles Press, Edinburgh, and one play *The Other Dear Charmer* published by Duckworth. Other of his plays exist only in manuscript. None of George Munro's plays has yet been published.

CONTEMPORARY WRITERS
Stewart Conn's work has been published by Calder and Boyars, as has Stanley Eveling's and Tom Gallacher's. Southside have published plays by Bill Bryden and Roddy McMillan, while Cecil Taylor has been published by a variety of publishers including Penguin and Scottish Theatre editions. The Molendinar Press has published Hector MacMillan's work and 7:84 scripts have been brought out by the West Highland Publishing Company and the Edinburgh University Student Publications Board and by Pluto Press.

THEATRES IN SCOTLAND DURING THE TWENTIETH CENTURY

IT IS NOT CLAIMED that the following list is totally accurate, but it is reasonably so. The list has been produced by combining information from various sources: town clerks, librarians, archivists, chief constables, the *Stage Provincial Guides* (1910, 1950, 1959-60), the *Kinematograph Year Book*, police records, newspaper files and associated materials. The list of necessity concentrates on theatres used primarily for professional presentations.

	Opened	*Closed*
ABERDEEN		
Her Majesty's Opera House/Tivoli	1872	1966
Palace	1898	1929
His Majesty's	1906	—
Beach Pavilion	1928	1961
ARBROATH		
The Theatre	c. 1890	1919
AYR		
Gaiety	1902	—
Pavilion	1911	1933
CLYDEBANK[1]		
Gaiety	pre-1900	1920
Pavilion	pre-1900	1919
COATBRIDGE[2]		
Theatre Royal	c. 1895	1920
COWDENBEATH		
Empire	1910	1914
DUNDEE		
Her Majesty's	1885	1919
Palace	1893	1911
Alhambra/Tivoli	1898	1929
Empire	1903	1911
Gaiety/Victoria	1904	1928
King's	1909	1928
Queen's	1922	c. 1928
Repertory Theatre[3]	1939	—

	Opened	Closed
EDINBURGH		
Gaiety/Operetta House	1875	1906
Lyceum	1883	—
Theatre Royal	1884	1946
Empire	1892	1962
Pavilion/Alhambra	1897	1921
Tivoli/Grand	1901	1920
King's	1906	—
Elm Row/Gateway	1931	1965
Palladium	1933	1966
Traverse [4]	1963	—
FALKIRK		
Grand	1903	1929
Electric/Empire/Roxy	1910	1958
GLASGOW		
Scotia/Metropole	1862	1961
Britannia/Panopticon	1870	1920
Her Majesty's/Royal Princess/Citizens'	1878	—
Royalty/Lyric	1879	1959
Theatre Royal [5]	1880	—
Grand	1882	1918
Queen's	1893	1951
Empire	1897	1963
Tivoli/Gaiety	1899	1909
Lyceum	1900	1929
Palace	1904	1947
Pavilion	1904	—
King's	1904	—
Coliseum	1905	1925
Hengler's Circus	1905	1925
Alhambra	1910	1969
Savoy	1911	1916
West End Playhouse/Empress/Metropole	1914	1969
Olympia	1920	1936
Park	1941	1949
Close	1965	1973
GREENOCK		
Theatre Royal/Hippodrome	1858	1923
Empire	1903	1958
Alexandria/King's	1905	1928
Palace/Pavilion	1905	1908
HAMILTON		
Hippodrome	1907	1946

	Opened	*Closed*
INVERNESS		
Theatre Royal	1882	1931
Music Hall	c. 1884	c. 1912
Empire	1934	1970
Eden Court	1976	—
KILMARNOCK		
Corn Exchange/Palace	1963	—
King's	1904	1929
KIRKCALDY		
King's	1904	1924
LEITH		
Gaiety	1889	1913
Alhambra	1914	c. 1918
MOTHERWELL/WISHAW		
New Century	1901	1913
Electric/Empire Electric	1911	1951
PAISLEY		
Theatre	1893	1959
Hippodrome	1906	1916
PERTH		
Repertory	1900	—
PITLOCHRY		
Festival	1951	—
RUTHERGLEN		
Repertory	1939	1959
ST. ANDREWS		
Byre [6]	1933	—
STIRLING		
Alhambra	1882	1939
MacRobert Centre	1971	

NOTES

1. Clydebank burgh library's records have no accurate information on theatres before 1912; it has therefore been assumed that both theatres existed in 1900.
2. A recent fire and consequent destruction of burgh records precludes more accurate dating.
3. Transferred to temporary premises in 1963.
4. Transferred to new premises in 1969.
5. Closed 1957; re-opened by Scottish Opera in 1975.
6. Transferred to new premises under same name in 1970.

INDEX